about
JENGA

about

JENGA

....

THE **REMARKABLE BUSINESS** OF **CREATING** A **GAME**
THAT **BECAME** A **HOUSEHOLD NAME**

....

LESLIE SCOTT

GREENLEAF
BOOK GROUP PRESS

Published by Greenleaf Book Group Press
Austin, TX
www.greenleafbookgroup.com

Distributed by Greenleaf Book Group LLC

For ordering information or special discounts for bulk purchases, please contact Greenleaf Book Group LLC at PO Box 91869, Austin, TX 78709, 512.891.6100.

Design and composition by Greenleaf Book Group LLC
Cover design by Greenleaf Book Group LLC

Publisher's Cataloging-In-Publication Data
(Prepared by The Donohue Group, Inc.)

Scott, Leslie (Leslie Ann), 1955-
   About Jenga : the remarkable business of creating a game that became a household name / Leslie Scott. -- 1st ed.

   p. ; cm.

   ISBN: 978-1-60832-002-8

1. Jenga (Game)--History. 2. Games--History. I. Title. II. Title: Jenga.

GV1469.J46 S36 2010
794   2009930305

Part of the Tree Neutral™ program, which offsets the number of trees consumed in the production and printing of this book by taking proactive steps, such as planting trees in direct proportion to the number of trees used: www.treeneutral.com

Printed in the United States of America on acid-free paper

14 13 12 11 10 09   10 9 8 7 6 5 4 3 2 1

First Edition

For Fritz and Freddie and Digby—in equal measure

CONTENTS

ACKNOWLEDGMENTS

I thank all at Greenleaf Book Group for steering me through this project with considerable expertise and great good humor; in particular, Bill Crawford, Jay Hodges, Linda O'Doughda, and freelancer Jeanne Pinault for their editing skills; Lisa Woods for her design flair; and Matt Donnelley for his guiding hands.

I also want to thank Bob Peirce, Fiametta Rocco, John Lloyd, John Mitchinson, Angela Palmer, and Richard Dawkins for connecting me, and Susan Moran for challenging me to dig deeper—then supporting me as I dug.

I thank my mother, Jo, for her unwavering belief in me. I thank my sister, Sue Macpherson, for her countless considerations and her nine photographs. Most of all, I thank my beloved husband, Fritz Vollrath, for everything.

INTRODUCTION

By any scale of reckoning, I think it fair to consider the game of Jenga a phenomenal success. Close to 50 million copies have been sold over the past twenty-six years. Few novel game ideas are ever turned into products that even make it to market. Very few that do make it to market last beyond a season or two, and very, very few of those become a household name worldwide. Jenga is one of these very, very few of the very few.

Though I am a professional game designer (one of few) and have researched, devised, published, and marketed close to forty games during the past twenty-six years (some original, some derivative, some more successful than others), I have always struggled to find an entirely satisfactory answer when asked to explain the secret of the appeal and success of Jenga, my first game.

This book is the result of my attempt to find this answer. In very many ways I think it can be read as the journal of a voyage of discovery—a traveler's tale, if you wish. Trying to understand why a rather simple idea I had in the seventies is a global cultural phenomenon today has felt to me much like traveling slowly and thoughtfully back up the wide and fast-flowing river I once rafted down at great speed.

I'm still not convinced that I have found the source of that river—a simple answer to Jenga's or my own success. I'm not even sure that

I have located the place where my original journey began. But on this leisurely reverse expedition I have discovered and explored some important tributaries and have spotted and charted many of the obstacles and rocks I must have instinctively dodged, skimmed, or tacked to avoid on that exhilarating original ride.

For example, though I consider myself a bit of a coward (I would never in a million years literally raft down an uncharted fast-flowing river on my own!), one of the most surprising discoveries I made on this envisioned rerun is that I took so many risks.

I left the security of a well-paid job with a great future, I risked my own and then my mother's home, I risked bankruptcy, I risked friendships, and I risked a great deal more besides. Even with hindsight, I'm not entirely sure why, though too timid to risk life and limb, I was fearless enough to put in jeopardy a very comfortable life, all for the sake of a game.

Perhaps, much as a strong rower, confident in his own abilities, might consider minimal the dangers of white-water rafting, I was so confident of Jenga that I calculated the risks I took as being little risk at all.

Or perhaps I was so determined to make a success of Jenga that, though perfectly aware of the magnitude of the stakes and what I stood to lose, I believed, on balance, that the risks were worth taking.

Or maybe curiosity pushed me to take these risks, as curiosity often does. Though much maligned (after all, we're warned that it killed the cat), curiosity is, I believe, what drives most human endeavor; it is the burning desire to find out what happened in the past, what is happening now, or what might happen if we take that next step.

Or possibly, taking chances is in my blood. I have always enjoyed playing games that offer a particular kind of challenge, ones that require imagination and ingenuity (brains rather than brawn) to overcome. But even this kind of challenge wouldn't be a challenge if there were not a significant element of risk, if there were not a real chance of failing or having to start all over again.

Whether for any or all of these reasons, I took the risks and even appeared to thrive on the continual challenge they offered. Perhaps rather tellingly, when I first launched Jenga, I called it "the perpetual challenge." I used the word *perpetual* (rather than *ultimate*, which is how it's described today) deliberately because I wanted to imply that the game continually presents new challenges. Every game is different. There is no single solution. You cannot conquer the game as such. Even when it comes crashing down, you can build a new tower and start again fresh. That, in my opinion, was and still is, in large part, the enduring appeal of the game.

Alhough the risks they are prepared to face might be different in kind, an explorer setting out on a journey, an entrepreneur initiating a new business, and a contestant starting a fresh game all love the thrill and the satisfaction that come from overcoming a challenge that demands sharp wits and presence of mind.

In many ways, playing a game is like starting and running a business, which in turn is like embarking on a solo journey down a swiftly flowing river. However experienced you may be, however carefully you plan your trip in advance, once you're out there being whooshed along by a powerful current, you will be confronted by unexpected obstacles rising up and potentially blocking your way. A propensity to see the way around, over, or through these obstructions and a penchant for the perpetual challenge will keep you speeding on your exciting voyage to success.

ONE

Building Blocks

People who know about Jenga are usually surprised when I tell them that I created the game. Many seem as incredulous as they would be if I had told them that I had invented the wheel. Having played it for years or, in some cases, so they tell me, "all my life"—which is entirely possible if they are under thirty—they assume Jenga has been around forever.

Why is this?

I think there is one very good reason, and this reason may also be one of the keys to understanding Jenga's success. This is that the game seems almost too *obvious* to have been designed with intent.

Children at play have probably piled block-like objects, one on top of the other, to create tower-like structures ever since block-like objects existed, which is probably as long as children at play have existed. Quite probably, they have also knocked down each other's blocks from time immemorial, too. So to have someone claim to be the first person to have devised a game that involves building a tower by piling wooden blocks on top of one another might seem just a little far-fetched to many people. And I can fully appreciate why. After all, it took me almost ten years from playing the first version of the game with my family in Ghana (circa 1973) to putting it on the market in London in January 1983, in part because it took me that long to realize that the idea was in any way novel.

Yet, as far as I am able to tell—and I have researched this pretty extensively—no game even remotely similar to Jenga existed before the early seventies.

The extraordinary claims about Jenga's provenance that I have come across are simply not true. For example, it was never played by the Chinese using perfectly crafted pieces of jade, however shattering (literally) that idea may be.

And it was not, emphatically not, an African game, played by generations of Ghanaians, though there are those who would contend that it was.

There are no illustrations of children or adults playing Jenga-like games from any culture at any period before now, and there is no mention of such a game in any literature, folklore, or anthology of games.

Stone, ivory, and glass dice; ivory, pottery, and sheep-knuckle counters; marble boards marked out for tabula (a Roman version of backgammon); and rows of holes scooped out of stone (for awari, a game that utilizes pebbles or beads) have been unearthed over all the world in, for example, Viking graves, Egyptian tombs, Roman ruins, and Benin palaces. But Jenga-like blocks have never been found, anywhere.

However counterintuitive this may seem, and however *obvious* it might appear in retrospect, over the millennia and across the world, no one seemed to have taken that *obvious* next step to formalize a game using little oblong building blocks.

No one had done that, that is, until I did, when I stepped forward with Jenga: a game with an African name that is not an African game. But it had its beginnings in Africa, so, perhaps then, the story of the remarkable business of creating this game should begin in Africa, too: specifically, in Dar es Salaam, Tanganyika, East Africa, on a Sunday in December 1955.

Natural Causes

Are when and where I was born relevant to this story of the origin of Jenga or its success as a game, or even to my own success as a game designer? Well, maybe. Certainly, many people argue that both nature (i.e., the genes you inherit from your parents and they from theirs) and nurture (when, where, and how you were raised) significantly influence the talents you have and the choices you make throughout life. So, perhaps a brief summary of my background and family might shed some light on how and why Jenga came about in the first place.

I was born in the Haven of Peace (Dar es Salaam), the bustling, noisy, hot, and humid coastal capital of what was then Tanganyika and is now Tanzania. This is where my parents were living in 1955 with their two-year-old son, Graham.

My father, Robert Howard Andrew Scott, had been an officer in the Royal Air Force and had fought as a Spitfire pilot during WWII. Although just twenty-two years old when the war ended, my father knew that after three adrenaline-fueled years spent airborne, coming back down to earth and returning to school was inconceivable. So was the idea of settling down to any of the deskbound jobs available to him in London. Throwing caution to the wind (he had no idea what he was going to do when he got there), he set off for Africa to seek a bright new life for himself, leaving his parents and four younger siblings behind in drab postwar Britain.

Although he had never set foot anywhere in Africa before arriving, first, in Kenya, my father was born and raised in the tropics—in the town of Syrian, Hanthawaddy, Burma, to be specific—where his father had spent many years as the chief engineer of Burma Oil. The war had cut right across any plans my father had had for following in his father's footsteps and becoming an engineer. Curiously, as things turned out, he did forge a successful career in the oil business, as his father had done.

My father was a remarkable man. Highly principled and conservative in many ways, he did not believe in moral gray areas; something was either right or it was wrong. Perhaps typically British in some respects, he had none of the European's usual prickly pride, and thus had little need to defend himself against what is foreign by instantly condemning it. On the contrary, he embraced and enjoyed the unfamiliar, and he had an infectious and anarchic sense of humor, with a great appetite for the quirky and fun. Africa suited Dad well. He considered life there an exciting adventure, and with him it was never frightening or dull.

I am not sure that it is an inheritable trait, but I do seem to have acquired much of my father's gung-ho-and-everything-is-possible attitude to life. And I am very grateful for that. It is fun. However, I regret that I didn't absorb more of the innate acumen he had in abundance. With his ability to assess, accurately, people and situations, Dad had a unique talent for taking the calculated risk that pays off.

There are many stories I could tell about my father to give you a flavor of the man who had such an influence on my life; the following is just one of my favorites. In the early fifties, much of Tanganyika was still sparsely populated. People living in the interior had seldom seen a white person, let alone a motorized vehicle. As a raw recruit for Standard Vacuum Oil, one of father's first jobs was to plan where to strategically site the country's first network of gas stations. For this, he had to drive from one tiny remote village to another, often tens or even hundreds of miles apart. Later, he traveled around the same villages to supervise the building of the stations he had planned. ("Stations" might be a little too grand a title, since most consisted of one hand-cranked gasoline pump and a locked room in which a few barrels of oil or diesel were stored.) Later still, he visited them on a regular basis to check on how they were being managed and run.

On one occasion, a year or so after the station had been installed, father turned up at a village way out in the middle of the *bundu*, the bush, to find that its fuel store was empty. The supply truck had been delayed en route by rain that within minutes had turned the dust roads into impassable quagmires. Even though the gas gauge in his car was on empty, my father recklessly decided to drive on to the next village, forty miles or so up the road, fearing he might otherwise be caught in the impending rains and stuck fast for weeks. He argued to himself that there was probably just enough fuel in the bottom of the car's tank to make the distance. He knew, however, that the fuel pipe did not reach to the bottom of the tank, so it would not be able to suck up all the gas. Using a jerrican he had asked a villager to fill from the village well, father carefully poured what he thought to be just enough water into the tank to cause the gasoline to float and to rise the requisite amount. He then quickly hopped into his car and drove off, luckily making it to the next village where there was still fuel. There he siphoned out the water, refilled the tank with gas, and motored back home to Dar es Salaam.

A couple of months later, on his next tour of inspection, Dad turned up at the village to be greeted by a very sour-faced station manager who told him that fuel sales had ground to a halt. So, too, had the only two cars in the village, and all the other vehicles that had driven through the village since the end of the rains. Word had quickly spread that people had witnessed with their own eyes my father pouring water into his car and driving away. If his car ran on free water from the village well, why couldn't theirs? Bwana Petroli had a great deal of explaining to do.

MY FATHER AND MY MOTHER, though quite different characters in many ways, shared a capacity to see innovative ways around problems. In my father's case, this came from an innate ability to sum up a situation and swiftly run through all possible solutions in the blink of an eye (a useful trait to have had as a Spitfire pilot). In my mother's case, her happy disposition meant that she often didn't acknowledge a problem as a problem in the first place and thus would make her way past it in happy ignorance, confident that all was well with the world. She is like this still.

Living in a small village in England as she does today, my mother can appear unconventional, if not mildly eccentric, but her independent and optimistic attitude to life equipped her well to cope in her natural environment, that is, Africa, where she was born and raised and lived until she left for Europe with my father when he retired.

My mother, Josephine Ann Masters, was born on Chiwanjee, a tea farm near Tukuyu in the Southern Highlands of Tanganyika. The story of this tea farm embraces the whole history of my maternal ancestors, the Masters family, generations of whom were born and raised in India. A distant cousin, the author John Masters, drew on this family's history in many of his historical novels set in India—*Bhawani Junction, The Night Runners of Bengal,* and others. Seven of these books portray members of successive generations of a fictitious British family serving in the British Army in India from the seventeenth century until the country's independence in 1947, as did successive members of the Masters family.

According to family lore, my mother's great-uncle, Alec Masters, a cavalry officer who fought in Afghanistan in the Battle of Kandahar in 1880 on the staff of Lieutenant-General Sir Frederick Roberts, had in old age retired from India to Cheltenham, England. Growing rather bored with this sedentary life, Alec persuaded his nephew (my mother's father) to join him in a farming venture in what had recently become the British Mandate of Tanganyika. Formally known as German East

Africa, it was here my grandfather had just spent much of WWI fighting in a campaign that the interested reader can explore in the darkly comic 1982 novel *An Ice-Cream War,* by William Boyd (Hamish Hamilton, London).

My grandparents trekked up from South Africa on horseback and on foot to join Great Uncle Alec on Chiwanjee, the farm he had bought, which was a failing coffee plantation at the time. My intrepid grandmother was to retrace this remarkable journey for "old times' sake" forty years later when she was almost eighty-five years old.

Though he had no direct farming experience, my great-great-uncle decided that the climate and the soil of the *shamba*, the farm, looked more conducive to growing tea than coffee. And, as it happened, through his old regiment he had the right to acquire tea seedlings (or seeds) from India. Apparently another member of the Masters family, while serving with the same regiment many years prior, had discovered wild tea in Assam, which had resulted in the rights to seeds of this tea bush being conferred on the whole regiment. Whether this part of the story is entirely accurate or not, the coffee plants were dug up and tea saplings were planted. As a consequence, my grandparents were some of, if not the, first people to grow tea in the Southern Highlands of Tanganyika, a region now famous for its tea. I say "grandparents," but more accurately should say "grandmother." Having decided and agreed on what needed to be done on the farm, my great-great-uncle and grandfather left my grandmother to dig up the coffee, plant the tea, and run Chiwanjee while they took off to pan for gold, which had recently been discovered along the Lupa River.

My mother was born on this very remote and isolated farm when both her father and great-uncle were away on this unsuccessful mission. The only "doctor" of the region who was called to assist my grandmother with the birth turned out to be a young veterinary surgeon. He had helped with the births of many other mammals but had never seen a human baby being born. After my grandmother had given birth, she asked the question all new mothers ask: "Is she all right?"

The vet replied, "Well, she seems to be . . . only—"

"Only what?" my grandmother asked frantically. "What's the matter with her? What's wrong?"

"Well, I'm not sure anything is wrong exactly. But she has her eyes open, which is rather precocious and strange."

My mother's early childhood was spent running around playing with children of the local Nyakyusu tribe on this remote and very beautiful farm overlooking Lake Nyasaland, until it was decided, to her great dismay, that she needed a "proper" education. She was sent first to the Belgian Congo, to a boarding school in a convent run by French-speaking nuns. Here she was, as she says, "incarcerated" for almost a whole year without seeing her parents. Although she became fluent in French, her abiding memory of "this prison" was being forced to eat dry bread spread with "cloggy" peanut butter, which she loathes to this day. Later, during WWII, Mum was sent to the Limuru School for Girls in the highlands of Kenya. Repressive by today's standards, the school was nevertheless an altogether jollier place than the convent. Here Mum made the firm friends who today still call her "Jam," the nickname they gave her from day one when she arrived at the school wearing an oversized sweater lovingly knitted by her sister, emblazoned with her initials, J.A.M.

After the war, my grandparents moved down to South Africa, where my mother spent her final school years in Pretoria. She then went on to study English at Rhodes University. She was never particularly happy in comparatively illiberal South Africa, and the enactment of apartheid laws in 1948 that institutionalized racial discrimination, which my mother abhorred, helped her decide that it was time to return "home," that is, to Tanganikya. My mother moved to Dar es Salaam to be with her married sister, who was fourteen years her senior and whom Mum adored. It was in Dar es Salaam that my parents met on a blind date (another calculated risk that paid off), fell in love, married, and had three of their four children.

SOON AFTER MY YOUNGER sister, Susan, was born, my parents moved us all (i.e., my older brother, my sister, and me) from Dar es Salaam to Kampala in Uganda, then to Nairobi in Kenya, then to Freetown in Sierra Leone (by which time my younger brother, Malcolm, thirteen years my junior, had been born), then back to Nairobi in Kenya, and finally, when I was turning seventeen, to Accra in Ghana. We lived in many different houses throughout my childhood, but somewhere in Africa was always home.

Sifting through my memories of growing up in Africa, what strikes me now is just how strange a mishmash are the cultural references for a family such as mine—that is, a family that has spent generations outside Britain yet still considers itself British at heart.

For example, in our case, most high days and holidays would be celebrated with colorful feasts of curries and rice (in Kenya) or groundnut stew with all the trimmings (in Ghana) and laid outside on long tables in the shade of the purple jacaranda or yellow thorn trees (in Kenya) or on the stone verandah under the whirling fans and hanging stag ferns (in Ghana). Mangoes and guavas and granadillas and pineapples and bananas would be chopped and diced and chilled and served with ice cream for the dessert.

But Christmas was always a very "traditional" English affair. Way before we children had experienced snow or ice, a tree, usually a rather spiky monkey-puzzle conifer, would be cut and brought into the house, sprayed white with fake snow, and have glass icicles dangled from its tropical branches. The Christmas cards we sent and received bore images of reindeer pulling Santa Claus across a snowy landscape, or a little red robin perched on a fork in a winter's garden, or rosy-cheeked children dressed in coats and scarves, building snowmen or skating on ice. And we would sit down indoors on what was invariably the hottest day of the year and eat a huge meal of roast turkey with all the trimmings, followed by a flaming Christmas pudding served with oodles of brandy butter. I wasn't too fond of this sweet sticky dessert but always ate plenty because it increased the chances of finding one of the silver sixpence pieces buried within. Though you couldn't spend this English coin anywhere in Africa, we all knew finding one would bring great luck—if you didn't swallow it accidentally, as I did once.

Following dinner, my father would tune the radio to the BBC World Service and we would all sit quietly "and no fidgeting" listening to Her Majesty the Queen, in her oddly clipped English accent (pronouncing *house* as "hice"), address all her loyal subjects, which, we had been told, included us.

As a small child, I always pictured the Queen sitting on a horse with a diamond-encrusted crown on her head giving this speech from Buckingham Palace (where I knew Christopher Robin had gone with Alice), a building I assumed must look much like the Muthaiga Country Club, the English Club, in Nairobi. Painted an ice-cream pink, this rambling colonial building with its highly polished wooden floors and uniformed staff was the most enchanting place I knew. In fact, with Kenya as my only reference point, I imagined London to be very much like Nairobi, only twinkling prettily with a dusting of ice and snow rather than a coating of fine red dust.

It was so utterly different from what I had expected that I recall in considerable detail my first visit to England. It was in December, and I was ten. Apart from the intense cold, and the novelty of seeing English people living in row upon row of houses built so close together, it was the first time I realized that if you wanted to see giraffes or zebras or elephants in England, you had to visit a zoo—a horrid place where the animals that roamed unfettered throughout much of Kenya paced up and down or hopped around tiny concrete cages behind bars.

I returned to Kenya with a sharper appreciation of my African home, as well as a somewhat deflated opinion of what it meant to be

British. I trust I had never consciously thought I was superior in any way—and I know my parents would have divested me of any such opinion if I had—but I am acutely aware that until I saw London for myself, I had assumed everything in Britain would be better than it was in Kenya, and it was humbling to find that it was not.

At age ten, I wouldn't have been able to say this in so many words, but I think what I had picked up on, and what I have seen evidence of many times since, is that the long-term expatriate either romanticizes the virtues of his home country at the expense of his adopted home, or he justifies his expatriate status (if only to himself) by overemphasizing the down side of life in his mother country or fatherland. Either way, I think, he loses a stranger's sense of perspective.

Perhaps this is why, though I now live on a farm in England, I still spend several months of the year on a ranch in Kenya. This way, though my roots might be shallow, familiarity isn't given a chance to breed contempt, and I don't risk losing sight of the merits of either country.

I love the history, the literature, the museums, the art galleries, the opera, the architecture, and the gardens of Great Britain. And I love its proximity to the rest of Europe, a complex continent with so much still to explore. And I love the astonishing landscape and the unique wildlife of Kenya and the warmth and the humor of the Kenyan people. Maybe I want the impossible. I want to have my cake and I want to eat it, too. I want to feel at home in England, and I want somewhere in Africa always to welcome me back home.

Play Up! And Play the Game!

Though not African in origin, it could be said that Jenga had its origins in Africa. For it was when we were living in Accra, Ghana, on the West Coast of Africa, that my family first played a version of the game that seven or eight years later I was to turn into a marketable product and name "Jenga," a word I borrowed from KiSwahili, a language of the East Coast of Africa. I would love to be able to pinpoint the precise eureka moment in which the game was fashioned from a collection of handmade wooden blocks, but I can't, because I don't think any such moment took place.

As far back as I can remember, my family played all sorts of games: generic games like chess, droughts (checkers), dominoes, backgammon, mah-jongg; published games like Scrabble, Clue, and Monopoly; traditional African games like mancala, bao, and awari (all versions of the same game); and party games, many of which we made up or adapted from old pastimes, our own version of charades and the dictionary game being particular favorites.

I don't know that we were an especially competitive family, though having said that, I'm not sure quite how to explain away a photograph I found recently. It's of me at my fourth birthday party finishing first in an egg-and-spoon race, which seems innocent enough until you look closely at the photograph and notice that the spoon I am holding is upside down and yet the egg is still in place!

When questioned about this, my mother unashamedly admitted that she had always glued the egg to the spoon because everyone deserved to win at least one race at her own birthday party. However shocking and thoroughly un-British her tactics had been, I wonder if this might explain why I have gone through life quietly confident that things will usually turn out all right—that, in a manner of speaking, the egg won't fall out of my spoon.

Whether excessively competitive or not, I think one of my family's defining, if perhaps quirkiest, traits was an almost compulsive habit of turning even the most unlikely activity into a competition or a game. Walking by flowing water invariably triggered our own versions of Pooh Sticks. The game as played by Winnie the Pooh involves players dropping sticks simultaneously into a river on the upstream side of a bridge, before dashing to the other side of the bridge to see whose stick is the first to appear. If a bridge wasn't available, we would decide on a beginning and a finishing point, and then play Pooh Leaves in gentle-flowing streams; Pooh Logs in wider, fast-flowing rivers; and Pooh Poo on occasion when sufficient elephant dung, which is very fibrous and floats like a dream, was at hand.

Any time we spotted the telltale signs of ant lions (or "doodlebugs")—the inverted conical lairs these insect larvae dig into sand or soft earth to trap ants—we would lie flat on our stomachs in a flash, each choosing a different "lion" to champion and to cheer on to successfully capture the most ants.

The long, shiny, hard-shelled African millipedes we found (common in woodlands on the Kenyan coast) were invariably encouraged to race each other. It's not the easiest thing to make them do, as they tend, if poked, to curl up in a ball and refuse to budge or, if on the move, veer wildly off course and battle or mate with one another.

Eating olives would invariably end up in a competition to see who could hit a glass set up as a target some feet away with an olive pit propelled by squeezing it between finger and thumb. Within minutes, rules would be suggested and agreed upon. Your arm could/couldn't be fully extended; if you hit the glass you scored one point, if it landed in the glass you scored two points, a point was deducted if the stone hit the cat sleeping nearby, etc.

Anyway, in such an environment it was hardly surprising that a collection of my younger brother's building blocks evolved into a stacking "game" of sorts, with little attention being paid to how or when this happened. All I can say with some certainty is that by 1974 my family was playing and enjoying a game using handmade wooden blocks made to order for us by a carpenter in Takoradi, Ghana's main port. Sets of these blocks, which we called "Takoradi Bricks," were presented in little wooden boxes and given by us as gifts to a handful of friends both in Ghana and back in the UK. In delving through my files to find material for this book, I came across some cuttings from the letters page of the *Oxford Times* of 1983 that I had long forgotten. The first letter is from a Mr. Euan Dunn inquiring about the origin of Jenga and mentioning how he had come across a game called Tako-radi Bricks at the home of the British High Commissioner in Accra in 1979. The second letter is my reply. Both letters (reproduced on page 125) are interesting and pertinent to the early history of Jenga, and Mr. Dunn's is particularly amusing and evocative of life as I remember it in Ghana from '72 to '76. Many evenings were spent in the home of the then British High Commissioner, Harry Stanley, and much time scouring for things in the markets of Accra.

As I've mentioned, some years were to pass before I jiggled with this early version of the game and came up with Jenga.

What I did throughout those years certainly shaped the direction of my future career as a game designer. I am not sure, though, that *career* is the right word; it seems to imply a course embarked upon more deliberately than the one I more or less fell into at the time.

TWO

An Unlikely Oxford Education

Like so many children of British expatriates dating back to the days of the Raj, from the age of thirteen my siblings and I were sent "home" to boarding school in the UK at the beginning of each term. We traveled back to Africa to spend the holidays at the end of each term. As a consequence, though I spent more than half of each year at my school in Somerset, England, I knew very little of the country—and nothing of the rest of Europe—before I left school and moved to Oxford.

I was an able enough pupil most of the way through school, even on occasions top of the class in some subjects, though never in French or Latin. Swahili was the only language other than English I've ever managed to speak with any fluency, and that's because I learned to speak it when I first learned to speak. Anyway, I picked up a goodly clutch of high grade O-levels, the first of two levels of standardized tests in Britain, at sixteen, and I like to think I might even have achieved reasonable results in my final-year exams if I had only put my mind to it, as my mother had urged me to do. As it was, by that time sorely distracted by life beyond the school gates, I actually failed every one of my A-levels, the exams I needed to pass to qualify for university. This was a notable achievement at my school, where *no one* else failed any A-levels and many of my peers were awarded the highest grades possible and went on to study at Oxford or Cambridge.

So rather than going on to university to study engineering and become the bridge builder I had always said I wanted to be, I went to college in Oxford to be trained as a teacher, notwithstanding the fact that teaching was the *only* profession I had always categorically stated I never wanted to follow. However, ever the pragmatist, toward the end of my last year at school, faced with the hard facts that I was about to fail my exams from too much fun and too little work far too late, and that I wouldn't otherwise be able to follow my good friends to Oxford, I convinced myself that teaching (I had discovered that no A-levels were required) would in fact suit me perfectly after all. Sadly, it did not.

Admittedly, I rather enjoyed the first two terms at the teacher training college when I was required to study the theory of education. We were introduced to the work of Swiss philosopher Jean Piaget, and I learned that the age group I was being trained to teach (seven- to eleven-year-olds) would be entering the "concrete operational stage." In this stage, children begin to think logically and grasp the concept of cause and effect (e.g., that pulling a brick out of a tower might cause it to collapse).

But the reality of putting all this theory into practice with real children in a real English primary school was an entirely different kettle of fish. I could see no evidence that these children had begun to think logically about anything at all, concrete or otherwise. However, I did discover they had an innate appreciation of cause and effect, which was very useful when, in an attempt to keep order in the classroom, I resorted to bribing my charges with sweets.

Scathing of my methodology, my supervisor suggested that teaching young children was a vocation for which I "appeared to have little calling" and it would be mutually beneficial if I were to consider using my "particular talents" elsewhere. He never specified what he felt were my particular talents or where they might be usefully employed, but then again, he didn't need to. I knew he was right—teaching was not for me. I left the college before the start of the second year.

Since devising rules turned out to be a specific talent of mine, it seemed a little ironic that what I disliked most about my brief teaching experience was having to enforce the school's rules. Of course, I don't mean each and every rule, just those that seemed arbitrary, or at least whose purpose appeared to me to have little to do with facilitating the children's education.

I can't say I thought too deeply about this at the time. After all, I was a recent escapee from a school myself, an institution where I had set about breaking almost every rule in the book. However, reflecting on this issue today, it occurs to me that perhaps much of my interest in playing games, devising games, and writing the rules for those games, is the clarity of purpose a game can offer.

It is funny how things can turn out. Many, many years after abandoning teacher training college, I ended up homeschooling our two children for several months at a time when my husband and I decided to live in the middle of the African bush, miles from any town or school.

I rather enjoyed this challenge and had even convinced myself that I was doing a reasonable job until my son, who was eight years old at the time, gently interrupted me one day, and asked, "Mum, I really don't mean to be rude, but exactly what *qualifications* do *you* have for teaching us? Do we *really* need to be able to tell a Burchell's zebra from a Grevy's zebra by the shape of its ears? Or a spotted hyena from a striped hyena by the sound of its laugh? And shouldn't we be doing French and Latin, not Swahili?"

Ouch! Perhaps the headmaster of his school in England had dripped doubt into my son's ear. When I went, cap in hand, to advise him that we would be taking our children out of school for yet another full term, the third year in a row we had done this, the headmaster, clearly enraged, had spluttered, "Good heavens, Leslie! I must say, I think that you and Fritz are exceedingly cavalier with your children's education!"

I replied indignantly, "Cavalier?! I think you need to define what you mean by *education*!" Incensed, I then launched into a tirade about how our children would be living with us among Masai herdsmen and Turkana warriors *and* world-renowned scientists on a research station in the middle of the African savannah where there is no electricity or television but where from the house you can watch elephants forage and wild dogs hunt dik-dik and see hornbills court each other on the verandah. Poor man. I am sure I said a great deal more before I finished by asserting, "Fritz and I are not being cavalier. Far from it. We believe that this *is* an education, and one worth giving our children while it's still possible to do so."

Saved by Jenga

In 1975, recognizing that I had none of the ability or patience necessary to encourage questioning children, I dropped any notion of becoming a teacher and went home to Ghana. I had a wonderful time exploring this culture-rich country, traveling inland along the Volta River and then crossing, by tiny crowded ferry, the vast Volta Lake, so recently formed by the Akosombo Dam that there were green leaves still on the tops of the trees we floated past at eye level. After several months of wandering about Ghana (at my parents' expense, I'm ashamed to confess), putting off even thinking about what to do next, I received a letter from Jerome Fletcher, a school friend now living in Oxford. Jerome invited me to accompany him and Chris Conlon, another school/Oxford friend, grape picking in Jerome's godmother's vineyard in France. I had never been to France and had never seen a vineyard, let alone picked grapes. It was an offer I simply couldn't resist.

Seeing a vineyard for the first time was quite a revelation. The only grape-bearing vine I had encountered was the huge one in the glass house in Hampton Court Palace, which we had visited on a school trip. As a result, I had envisaged that picking grapes would involve strolling under hanging vines leisurely plucking at fruit just above my head. Certainly, I had not imagined having to bend nearly double over squat bushes for hours at a time.

The work was grindingly hard, but it was made perfectly bearable because we were very well rewarded, both in French francs and in flagons of wine. Each day we worked virtually nonstop from eight until noon, broke for two hours, and then worked again from two until six. During the midday break, we would dash to the *mas*, the one-room farmhouse we three shared with Jean, Jerome's godmother's son, and eat a hearty meal of bread and cheese, which we washed down with vast quantities of wine. We would then sleep (pass out) for an hour. The afternoon shift passed in a pleasant haze, and before we knew it, we were back at the mas and stepping out of our overalls, which had become so stiff with dry grape juice that they would stand upright where they were left, ready for us to step back into them the next morning. We then poured ourselves yet more wine. While the evening's cook prepared dinner, the other three ambled about—reading, writing, playing games, and drinking more wine. I had brought a set of Takoradi Bricks with me and it became a firm favorite.

One evening during our second week in France, Jean was on dinner duty. Jerome, Chris, and I had started a game of Takoradi Bricks, but exhausted, hungry, and most likely tipsy, we had postponed finishing the game. We had left the tower of bricks—some thirty or so layers high, leaning gently to one side—atop the dining table in the middle of the room and had wandered off to relax on our beds, which lined the edges of the room.

I drifted in and out of sleep as I waited for Jean to call us to dinner. Suddenly, I came fully awake with a start. Across the room, Jean was attempting to replace the gas canister of a small gas lamp (the mas had neither power nor running water) by the light of a naked candle flame. I heard a loud pop followed by an angry hiss and realized with a shock that Jean had pierced the canister before attaching it to the lantern top. Gas, under considerable pressure, escaped and was instantly set alight by the candle. A huge jet of fire streaked across the room toward me, knocking over the tower of bricks that stood in its way.

"*Merde!*" Jean yelled, dropping the flaming canister and sprinting out of the building. Meanwhile, I had leapt up, instinctively scrambling to climb out the window to get out of the way. Looking back as I hooked my left leg over the edge, I was extremely puzzled to see, by the light of the flame, Jerome swinging from the velvet curtains that divided the kitchen off from the sitting-cum-sleeping area (I later realized he was trying to pull the curtains down to smother the fire) and then amazed to see Chris leap upon and grasp the flaming canister and fling it past my head and out of the open window. The canister landed in the vineyard, hissing and twisting and turning like a giant Catherine wheel that has spun away from its fixing. Stunned, I remained half in and half out of the window. Jean, Chris, and Jerome gathered by the door, and in dazed silence we watched the display until it spluttered to an end.

"*Mon Dieu!*" Jean gasped, breaking the silence. "*Quelle exposition!*"

"Yes, absolutely *vraiment*, what a show!" Jerome agreed. "Er, anyone need another little drink?"

Back in the mas, still a little shell-shocked, I gathered up the blocks that had scattered across the room when the tower had been blasted over, noticing as I put them back in their box that several had been badly scorched. It struck me that but for those blocks, which must have deflected the flame, I could have been quite seriously burned.

The Nubile Waitress

Unscathed and considerably wealthier, we all returned to Oxford, where Jerome and I and two other old friends from school, Bob Peirce and Judith Morgan, rented a house for a year. During this time, Bob and Jerome were both undergraduates at Oxford. Bob in his third year was reading History at St. Catherine's College, and Jerome in his second year was reading French and Spanish at Trinity College. At the start of the year, Judith was working for a headhunter in Oxford and I was still trying to decide what I wanted to do with my life. I spent the first six months trying a variety of projects, among which was teaching myself how to macramé, which was all the rage at the time. After a great many hours engaged in twisting and knotting bits of string, I managed to create some passably functional beaded hangers to hold baskets.

I sold my first batch of hangers to a small outlet on the Cowley Road and my second to a gas station in the tiny village of Curry Rivel in Somerset, run by one of the many grateful patients of Jerome's mother, who was a much-loved, if a little feared, district nurse. Flushed with success, I decided to teach a macramé class at The Old Fire Station art center in Oxford. To my considerable surprise, a group of ten women and one man appeared on the first day, and then every Wednesday morning thereafter for the eight weeks I ran the course. They seemed perfectly happy to practice tying the one knot over and over again in the first hour of the class, stop for coffee and biscuits, and resume knotting fifteen minutes later, when I had them work on a specific project. By the end of the eight-week course, my pupils departed knowing how to tie eight different knots and having each completed one almost identical basket hanger. They seemed satisfied with my class. In truth, I believe they probably enjoyed each other's company and my choice of biscuits as much as learning to macramé.

Pretty soon, I got rather bored of knotting, especially as it earned me very little and I was unable to find an outlet willing to take any more rope basket hangers, lamp shades, or belts. However, many years later my interest and moderate skill were revived in this subject when I designed a game called The Sailor's Knot, inspired by a wonderful book I had come across by Clifford Ashley, *The Ashley Book of Knots* (Doubleday, Doran and Co., Inc., 1944), which describes and illustrates how to tie more than thirty-eight hundred knots. Mr. Ashley records that although it took him eleven years to research the book, he believes that there were still old knots unrecorded and new knots to discover. Luckily for me, this book was not in wide circulation until long after my stint as a teacher of just the eight knots.

Casting about for something more lucrative to do while I considered my long-term future, I saw an advertisement for a waitress position at a new restaurant called Browns. I went for an interview, and despite my total lack of experience, I was offered the job, which I very nearly turned down when I was told the pay would be £12 per week, £1 less than I was paying for my share of the rent. "However," my interviewer told me, "you may keep all your tips, and believe me, *you* will be perfectly satisfied with how much you will take home," he added as he looked me up and down.

Sure enough, within two weeks I was taking home around a hundred pounds a week, which was a fortune at that time. He was right; I was perfectly satisfied, particularly as the earnings were undeclared and therefore untaxed.

Less than a month after opening their Oxford branch (they already had one in Brighton), Browns was considered a phenomenal success. Customers, students in the main, queued down the road and around the corner into Little Clarendon Street to get a table. They loved the atmosphere: French bistro–style, polished round tables, hanging plants, ceiling fans, the very loud music, and the food—good quality, inexpensive, and tasty. At that time, there had never been a restaurant quite like it in Oxford, and there were rave reviews, including the following, which appeared in the *Oxford Times*: "Browns' nubile waitresses are restaurant's main attraction."

I still meet people who are more impressed by the fact that I was a Browns' waitress back in '75 than by anything I have done since, which is odd when you consider that almost every woman will by definition have been nubile (i.e., of marriageable age) at some time in her life, but few will have gone on to design games.

I remained working happily at Browns for several months before the novelty began to wear off. I realized that however efficient I was as a waitress, I had reached the limit of what I could earn in tips in a week because I had reached the absolute limit of the number of customers I could serve in that period. As with my macramé venture, I had been excited at the prospect of facing a new challenge, of doing something I had never done before, but I had grown weary with the enterprise once there seemed little more to be learned.

By the time I left Browns, Judith had moved on from her headhunter's job to work as the personal assistant to the managing director of the UK division of Intel Corporation. Knowing I was getting low on cash, she offered me a temporary job helping her with some paperwork. I gratefully accepted, but I did so with very little expectation of finding the work either exciting or particularly challenging. I thought I would be there for a week or two at the most.

As it turned out, I ended up working for Intel for almost four years; the challenges just kept on coming. If I hadn't taken that initial temporary job at Intel, I doubt that I would have ever gained the marketing experience or the self-confidence necessary to launch Jenga or to start any business of my own.

THREE

Intel Inside

For three years in Oxford, a city world famous for its ancient university, its beautiful buildings, its "dreaming spires," Intel UK occupied a few uninspiring little offices above the Potato Marketing Board in a drab three-story sixties building situated on Between Towns Road in Cowley. So incongruous was this location that neither "gown" (the university) nor "town" (the rest of the Oxford inhabitants) appeared to notice this cuckoo in their midst, quietly hatching a revolution so profound that it would penetrate and change every single aspect of their daily lives. In 1979, when wanting to build its own office, Intel was told by the City Council that Oxford was "full" and it would be impossible to find space to accommodate it, so the company moved on to Swindon, once home of the Great Western Railway.

Today, if Oxford City's councilors are even aware of their predecessors' decision to turn away Intel, they must be kicking themselves. The German-owned BMW plant, all that remains of the once massive British Leyland Cowley car works, now builds just the one small car, the Mini, no doubt with "Intel inside." This employs just forty-five hundred people—thirty thousand fewer than twenty years ago, before robots with Intel inside took over the jobs. Oxford (both town and gown) is turning itself inside out to re-brand itself and attract home-grown and international high-tech companies to its purpose-built science and business parks. And few are more high-tech than the Intel Corporation, the one that they let slip away.

There were just six people working at the Intel office when I took the temporary job. I, like the majority of the world, had never heard of a microprocessor, let alone Intel, the company that invented it.

Absolutely fascinated by what I found they were doing, and inquisitive by nature, I couldn't stop asking questions.

Probably to stem my constant "What?" "Why?" "How?" and "Wow!" I was rapidly promoted from an envelope-stuffing temp to a full-fledged employee charged with the responsibility of starting and running a technical literature library to bring under control and disseminate the mass of information coming out of Intel's head office in Santa Clara.

A few months later, I became the contact point for Intel's PR consultant, the press, and anyone else interested in learning about Intel. And one year later, I was further elevated to be Intel UK's marketing communications manager, a position and title invented to describe the job I had been doing by default. Despite the fact that I was barely twenty-two and had no prior computing, marketing, or public relations qualifications, by 1978 I was managing all of Intel's promotional and PR activities in the UK and attempting to handle the seemingly insatiable demand for information about microcomputers in general and Intel products in particular. It was challenging and exhilarating and I loved the job, despite the odd scary moment or two of feeling a little out of my depth.

One such moment was toward the end of my first year with the company when Keith Chapel, the managing director, walked into my office and asked me to stand in for him as host to two very senior executives from Barclays Bank who would be visiting that day. He explained that the "banker guys" wanted to hear from "the horse's mouth" what long-term impact, if any, microprocessors would have on UK industry and business.

I wasn't at all sure I had the gravitas these city gentlemen would be expecting. When I voiced these concerns, Keith replied: "Who knows what a London banker's image is of the managing director of an electronics company. I think they would be surprised enough to find me at the helm, so why not totally unsettle them and insist they take seriously a twenty-two-year-old girl in a miniskirt?!"

His reply offered little reassurance, and I said as much.

"Don't worry," Keith said. "Meet them when they get off the train and whisk them off to that amazing new restaurant in Summertown everyone is talking about, Les Quat'Saisons. I know Raymond Blanc, the owner, from his Rose Revived pub days. He's a fantastic chef. A creative genius. I'm sure he'll go far. I'll ring him now and ask him to keep a special eye on you and to have some chilled champagne ready and waiting. Trust me. They'll be bowled over by Raymond, by you, and most important, of course, by what you have to teach them about Intel."

Waiting at Oxford Station for the train to arrive, any concern I had had about being able to identify my charges vanished the moment I spotted two elegant, clean-shaven, gray-haired men step out of a first-class carriage. Each wore gold-rimmed glasses, a crisp white shirt, a pinstripe suit, and polished black shoes. It was the seventies; flared jeans and long hair were de rigueur in Oxford for students and dons alike. I approached these two men from another world and introduced myself, telling them that Keith had asked me to greet them.

"How very kind," they both said pleasantly.

"Please, follow me. I have a taxi waiting just outside."

Once we had settled into the cab and were on our way, one of the men said, "I assume Mr. Chapel will be joining us there?"

"Well, actually he has asked me to send his apologies. He has been unavoidably detained and has requested that I look after you today and answer any questions you may have."

Disconcertingly, both men turned from gazing out of the window to focus on me as if seeing me properly for the first time.

"Really, dear? May I ask what position you hold in the company, Miss . . . mmm . . . Miss?"

"Scott, but please call me Leslie. I'm the data coordinator, er . . . manager," I replied, blushing and giving myself a quick promotion.

"A data manager? I see," he said slowly, pronouncing *data* to rhyme with *garter* rather than *greater* as I had done.

It was even worse than I had expected. I had not bargained on suppressed fury. To make matters worse, it turned out that Les Quat'Saisons was located right next to the headquarters of the famine relief charity Oxfam. Africa was suffering a drought of catastrophic proportions that year and Oxfam's windows were filled with giant posters of severely undernourished children. It seemed an inappropriate setting to indulge in a lavish meal to appease two well-fed bankers, to say the least.

Sighing, I opened the door and led the way into the small, stylishly dark restaurant. I was relieved to be greeted by Monsieur Blanc, ready with a bottle of champagne. As we sipped on the champagne and read the menu, I broke the silence by asking what their interest in Intel might be. It came as an immense relief to find that, irrespective of their senior positions and presumably extensive knowledge of the financial world, neither man had more than a very rudimentary idea of what a microprocessor was, let alone how it might be used. They had heard that computers were getting smaller and would become more affordable and that this had something to do with silicon chips. After eleven months at Intel, reading the literature I was processing, I found I had a doctorate in the subject by comparison.

"Tiny intelligent computers, etched into chips of silicon no bigger than your thumbnail, will be at the heart of every machine, from cars to toasters. Even banking will be turned upside down." I finished with a flourish.

Having at first sat rigid with disapproval, both men appeared to relax a little toward the end of the second glass of champagne (accompanied by some delicious canapés). By the time they were tucking in to the roasted loin of lamb, two courses and many glasses of a full-bodied red later, they had become chatty and friendly, and when we moved on to the dessert and a glass of sauterne, they were positively mellow. I popped a spoonful of heavenly meringue into my mouth breathing a sigh of relief that Keith's plan had worked and everything had turned out just fine. It was a bad move.

Sighing and meringue do not mix. I started to choke. To my horror, crushed meringue projected out of my mouth with an astonishing force, spraying the bankers with tiny pieces of sticky white foam. I leapt up, still coughing and spluttering and made a dash for the ladies' loo, mortified at what I had done. I stayed there a considerable time after I had stopped coughing, as I had no idea how to begin to apologize for such a gross display. I prayed feverishly that they had managed to remove all traces of meringue from their beautiful and expensive clothes.

When, finally, I came out and crept back to my seat, I was astounded to find the two men laughing and joking and on to coffee and brandy, apparently oblivious to what had happened. Not a single word was said about my coughing fit and when, nearly an hour later, they boarded the London-bound train, thanking me profusely for "an absolutely—hic—splendid and informative day," there were still pieces of meringue stuck in their hair, on their ties, their shirts, their suit jackets and, worst of all, pebble-dashed across their gold-rimmed specs.

Although the effusive thank-you note I received a few days later made no reference to this incident, to this day I will not eat meringue in public unless I am with very good or very drunk friends. At one time I would have said that this was the only useful lesson I learned from this particular encounter. However, in the process of writing this book and thinking about anything and everything that might in any way have contributed to building Jenga, the brand, I have begun to wonder if perhaps there were less palpable but important lessons I absorbed that day that I may have drawn upon, albeit unconsciously, and which may have influenced my approach to business.

For example, having recently read a biography of Robert Noyce, who with Gordon Moore founded Intel, it occurs to me that in asking a young girl to represent him that day, Keith had not been quite as imprudent as I had assumed; rather, he had been perpetuating the progressive and pioneering image Noyce had purposely set out to create for Intel.

As the general manager of Fairchild Semiconductor, where he had invented the integrated chip, and then at Intel, where he oversaw Ted Hoff's invention of the microprocessor, Noyce deliberately introduced a very casual, almost anarchic working atmosphere. He believed that only by giving young, bright employees the opportunity and the creative space to express themselves and accomplish what they wished would Intel attract the right people and keep ahead in a highly competitive and innovative field. It has been said that in many ways creating what became known as "the Silicon Valley working style" was as much a revolution as introducing the microprocessor. This is probably a bit of an exaggeration, but it can't be denied that it certainly had its effect, and when I come to think of it, it's a pretty impressive example of carefully considered corporate branding.

A final postscript to this tale: Keith was right—Raymond Blanc did go far. He's right there at the top, a celebrity chef with a television show, *Le Manoir aux Quat'Saisons Hotel*, and two Michelin stars to his name. In linking the cutting-edge company, Intel, with the innovative, rising star Blanc, Keith created an association in the minds of those bankers that I am sure they have never forgotten. They didn't notice the sticky meringue, but the sense of ingenuity and creativeness will have stuck. This, I now appreciate, was a masterful example of reinforcing the reputation of a brand.

Chips with Everything

Of the four years I worked for Intel, three were spent in its offices in the Potato Marketing Board building. As its communications manager, it was my responsibility to disseminate information about Intel's revolutionary products across the board. I believed I was doing a pretty good job. Two years after I had been in the position, I was brought up short. One day, in the elevator on my way up to the third floor, a fellow passenger, a young woman, asked, "So what do you guys do up there?"

"Intel? You mean what does the company do?"

"Yeah. In Tel? Are you in telephones?"

"No, not telephones. Computers and microchip technology."

"You make microchips?!" she exclaimed as she stepped out on to the second floor, the Potato Marketing Board's office. "That's amazing!"

I thought no more about this exchange. I was used to people getting excited about Intel's products. So I was very surprised when, a few days later, this same young woman came into my office dragging a large hessian sack.

"Potatoes," she said before I could ask. "A new variety of small potatoes that we would like you to test when you have the chance."

"Test?"

"Yes, please test them. We would like to know if they will make good micro chips."

Embarrassing though it was at the time, this misunderstanding taught me that to communicate effectively, you must be aware and take account of different experiences and perspectives. Different expectations, too, as I was to discover.

AS INTEL RAPIDLY EXPANDED worldwide, my responsibilities also expanded and grew to include organizing and promoting a series of traveling seminars, or road shows, that Intel took around the British Isles. We "played" to packed houses always, wherever we went. Engineers were thirsting for information about microprocessors, keen to incorporate them into their own company's products. At first, I assumed that, with engineers as our target audience, we should come across as sober, serious academic types, seemingly indifferent to such frivolous things as our surroundings and the quality of the lunch.

It was made clear soon enough, however, that in coming to learn about Intel's revolutionary products, these engineers expected all aspects of the day to be distinctive, exciting, and fun. They didn't want to sit in bland surroundings to learn about computers etched into silicon chips, however thrilling the topic, and they didn't want to eat the ubiquitous English pub fare of battered fish or chicken served with a basket of chips, however perfectly fried the potato. Once I appreciated this, I made sure that whenever possible our shows took place in five-star venues and the food was exotic or delicious, or preferably both.

As a kind of grand finale to wrap up a year of these traveling events, it was decided that we would hold one big, daylong event called "The Intel Fair," the organization for which landed on my desk. Mindful of what I had learned from the smaller events, I booked an ultramodern, five-star London hotel in which to hold the fair, which consisted of a succession of simultaneous seminars given by Intel's star personnel, including Robert Noyce and Gordon Moore, an exhibition of the latest equipment, and a spectacular three-course lunch, of course.

Five hundred people attended. It was declared a roaring success, and we decided to repeat it the next year on an even grander scale—this time hiring the brand-new Wembley Conference Centre complex and holding six simultaneous seminars and an enormous exhibition. I employed the Oxford design company Arena to design and build the exhibition and produce all the publicity material for the event, which they did with considerable flair, taking literally the word *fair* and focusing on a fairground theme with bunting, sideshows, merry-go-rounds, and all. One thousand and five hundred engineers *paid* to attend the event, and they left in high spirits and with up-to-date information about microcomputers, along with old-fashioned sticks of sweet, sticky fairground rock with the name INTEL running through the middle in blue. Misunderstandings about potato chips aside, perhaps this baton-shaped candy souvenir beloved of the British holidaymaker is the only edible product to have had "Intel inside."

Playing Games

Intel's European headquarters were in Brussels, which I visited regularly to meet with my counterparts to plan PR and advertising campaigns. I also attended the European sales conferences held twice a year in different European locations: chic Italian ski resorts in the main, as most Intel employees were passionate skiers. Apart from unintentionally providing much mirth at my ludicrous attempts to ski—there hadn't been much opportunity for me to ever try this particular sport in Africa—my primary role at these conferences was to outline the UK's promotional campaigns and to devise effective ways of helping the European sales teams keep abreast of Intel's ever-expanding product range.

Expecting salesmen—and they were *all* men at the time—to read dry, technical product descriptions did not work, despite the fact that every one of them was an electronics engineer and therefore, presumably, perfectly capable of understanding the content. Competition and making money, loads of money, were what motivated these men. So I devised games for them to play, competitive team games, with substantial cash or equivalent prizes for the winning team, that involved testing the players' knowledge of the company's products. The games were played after dinner, while they enjoyed a fine cognac and Cuban cigars. The relaxed, convivial atmosphere totally concealed my didactic agenda and belied the intense competitions taking place. And for me, creating these games was a genuine pleasure, a natural extension of a lifelong passion I had had for inventing and playing games—the cerebral kinds at least.

It's not that I was awful at all physical sports; I swam and played lawn tennis for my school in my teens. It's just that I was never athletic enough to achieve much satisfaction from playing games that required great agility, speed, or strength. Nevertheless, there was one exception, and that was Real Tennis, the forerunner of the game of lawn tennis. As much a game of strategy as it is a game of physical skill, Real Tennis—with its unique handicap system—enables players of very different levels of ability to play and to enjoy it. From the moment I first encountered it, Real Tennis had me in its thrall, and, as it happened, in a roundabout manner, this ancient game was the catalyst that set in motion the process of bringing to market the entirely new game of Jenga.

FOUR

Real Tennis and Flappy Ducks

Real, Royal, or Court Tennis, or Jeu de Paume, as it is known variously in the countries where the game is still played (Britain, the United States, Australia, and France) is the medieval forerunner of lawn tennis. With just forty-six Real Tennis courts left in the world, part of the appeal of playing this esoteric game is the access it grants to some very exclusive, exotic locations. Almost every extant Real Tennis court is attached to a historically remarkable property. for example, Merton College in Oxford, Hampton Court Palace in London, and the Georgian Court University in New Jersey.

Real Tennis players, and Real Tennis professionals in particular, are a pretty rare and arcane breed, too. This was something I found myself in a unique position to judge. After graduating from Oxford, Jerome (my boyfriend since school) took a job as the university's Real Tennis professional to manage its club on Merton College Lane, the narrow, cobbled, gas lamp–lit street that runs parallel to the wide and bustling main road that Oxonians call "The High." In doing so, he became one of a small handful of people ever to have earned a living from playing Real Tennis.

It was a singular choice of job for a modern language graduate, but then Jerome made a habit, even a fine art, of doing the exceptional. There cannot be many people who can list on their curriculum vitae elver fisherman, Real Tennis professional, published children's author, Venetian gondolier, director of performance writing at a college, and coauthor of three bizarre books on decadence (*The Decadent Gardener, The Decadent Cookbook*, and *The Decadent Traveller*), which led directly to him performing at a festival of decadent art in Bregenz, Austria, dressed in a beautifully tailored full-length coat made of thinly sliced pieces of Austrian smoked ham, "The Speckmantel," while his audience dined on fois gras.

Jerome's skill and passion in his miscellaneous and diverse interests are highly infectious. I owe to him the rare pleasures of having fished for silver elvers (baby eels) on the River Parrot by moonlight, of having punted a Venetian boat up the River Thames on a midsummer's day, of cycling through the walled cities of Cervantes's Spain . . . and, of course, of being introduced to Real Tennis and the unusual people who play this extraordinary game.

Two such are Chris Ronaldson and his wife, Lesley. Chris, the Singles World Champion from 1981 through 1987, was the professional attached to the Royal Tennis Court at Hampton Court Palace in London. He and Lesley, herself a champion, lived in an apartment within the grounds of this beautiful Tudor Palace built by Cardinal Wolsey. The Royal Tennis Court is the oldest court still in use in the world and the only one of the twenty-seven in Britain that admits the general public to watch when this ancient game is being played.

Visiting the Ronaldsons with Jerome for lunch one day, I leapt at the opportunity to take a lesson with Lesley. After barely ten minutes on court, I was exhausted. Lesley had had me dashing from one side to the other, chasing after balls she had effortlessly placed in alternate corners. Concentrating hard, I had failed to hear a group of tourists come in and sit down in the visitors' gallery situated alongside the court, only realizing they were there when, missing a ball, I paused near the gallery gasping for breath.

"Before he grew fat and gouty, the Tudor King Henry VIII was a passionate tennis player. It is believed he had this court built around 1528," the sonorous, authoritative voice of a tour guide rang out. "And legend has it that he was on court here in May 1536 when he received news of the death of his wife, Anne Boleyn, the mother of the future Queen Elizabeth the first."

"How did she die?" a young American girl asked.

"She was executed. She had her head cut off in the Tower of London."

"How awful!" the girl said.

"Indeed. Since Henry VIII to the present day, members of the Royal Family have enthusiastically played what we now call *real* tennis to distinguish it from its modern offshoot, *lawn* tennis. King Charles I, King George IV, Prince Albert, King Edward VII, and King George V have all supported the game and played it here. The current Prince Edward plays it here today. This is why this is called the *Royal* Court.

"Now ladies and gentlemen, if you will follow me . . ."

Lesley and I had resumed playing, and I was back trying to scoop up a ball near the gallery wall as the visitors started to file out of the building. As they passed nearby I heard a girl ask her mother, "Mom, did I understand her correctly? Did the tour lady say you have to be *royal* to play this game on this court?"

"That's what she said, honey."

"Gee."

Gee indeed, I thought, wondering which members of the Royal Family they thought Lesley and I might be.

Though I certainly felt fortunate in having been given the chance to enjoy this most regal of games, it had never crossed my mind that playing it might be an ennobling experience, literally. I didn't have a royal or any other title back then and I don't have one today. But of the myriad games I have played over the years, Real Tennis is undoubtedly the one to have exercised the greatest influence over my life. I met my husband through Real Tennis, and in many respects, it was because of the game of Real Tennis that I became a professional designer of games.

BUT BACK TO JEROME. At Oxford's Merton College, Jerome's job involved the many tasks common to all tennis club professionals— teaching players, umpiring matches, stringing rackets, etc.—and some unique to *real* tennis, hand-fabricating all the balls, for one. This arduous task involves sewing strips of woolen melton cloth around a wine cork encased in tightly wrapped cotton ribbon. I found myself spending more and more evenings after work in the professional's room at the club, sipping wine and binding and sewing balls to help Jerome keep up with the demand. It was on one such evening in early 1982 that some of the Oxford Club members asked if I might help organize a fund-raising event. Although the Merton College court is comparatively modern, only dating back to 1798 and the reign of King George III, there had been Real Tennis courts in Oxford since 1595. I used this fact to justify holding a Courtly Elizabethan Feast—this, and the fact that the inside of the building looks more sixteenth than eighteenth century, with its matte black walls, bright red markings, and regal white unicorn painted on its back wall.

Matte black walls, by the way, are a common feature of Real Tennis courts, though I suspect they are no longer painted as they once were with buckets of oxen blood and ox gall, diluted with lampblack and red wine.

I suggested holding the feast in the cavernous court itself, something I am certain the university would forbid today for health, safety, and insurance reasons. But it was approved without hesitation at the time. In preparation for the feast, the net was removed from the center of the court and planks were laid along the central guttering (into which balls hitting the net fall during play) to prevent anyone tripping in the atmospheric but somewhat shadowy candlelight I had planned for the court. Long tapestry-covered refectory tables and wooden benches were set up to accommodate the diners. Caterers served wine in goblets and roasted pork, beef, and venison on platters I hoped would pass as pewter in the semidarkness. Musicians and singers, fire-eaters, stilt walkers, conjurers, and jesters moved around the room among the guests as they ate and drank, and gaming stalls were set up around the perimeter of the court where bona fide Elizabethan games of skill and chance could be played, such as shove ha'penny, shovelboard, knuckels, and dice. And into this section I rather cheekily slipped my entirely modern game of bricks, claiming to anyone who asked—and few did—that it could genuinely be described as Elizabethan having been conceived during the reign of an Elizabeth, only in this case it was the current Elizabeth Regina rather than the first.

I can pinpoint the exact moment I decided that I would put my brick game on the market to the morning after this successful and noisy fund-raiser. Over the previous seven or eight years, I had witnessed many friends and family members enjoying it and had, as I've mentioned, had several sets handmade to give away. But until watching it that night captivate and enthrall a crowd of professional games players, it had not occurred to me that I might develop and market the game as a product. As I sat propped up in bed drinking a cup of coffee, ostensibly reading the Sunday newspapers though actually lost in reverie, it dawned on me that I could, and I should, and I would start a business and bring this game to market—and I did, starting the very next day.

Manufacturing Good

About a year before this pivotal Sunday morning, I had left my job at Intel to work for Arena, the design company I had commissioned to help me with the Intel Fair. Arena had offered me a substantial raise in salary, but what had actually persuaded me to leave Intel was that the directors of Arena had proposed creating a new position in the company specifically for me. As they had only recently ventured into the exhibition world, they offered me the post of marketing manager, responsible for developing this side of their business. I would be starting from scratch and could make of the position what I wanted. I found this idea fresh, exciting, and seductive at a point when my job with Intel had become comparatively staid. Whereas I had once felt positively encouraged to fly solo and by the seat of my pants, as Intel had grown and matured and management systems had been put in place, I had begun to feel rather constrained by having to plan, budget, and report. It wasn't that I didn't understand why I should be asked to account for what I was doing; it was just that having to do so took the edge off the *fun* that came from having the freedom to operate in my own way and make decisions I knew would be relevant.

I suspect that underpinning the many motives I may have had for starting each subsequent new venture since Intel—moving to Arena, taking Jenga to market, founding Oxford Games, and even writing this book—there is a quest to recapture that fun I experienced when I worked for Intel during those early, pioneering years.

Several excellent carpenters and cabinetmakers worked for Arena. One of them, Pat Cooke, had become a particular friend. On the Monday morning after the Real Tennis event, I took my box of bricks to show him and to ask for his advice about how it might be possible to mass-produce the bricks.

I had by this stage already developed the game beyond its first version, which had simply utilized the collection of wooden building blocks handmade in Ghana. I had altered the overall dimensions of each block so that its width was now exactly a third of its length. This meant that at the start of play, a sturdy tower could be built by tightly stacking layers of bricks three by three, each layer laid at right angles to the layer below. There was no need to place the blocks on edge and leave a gap between each block as had been necessary with the original blocks, whose widths were a little less than a third of their length. I had also added the rule, essential to the game that became Jenga, which requires a player to place the block she had just removed in her turn back on top of the tower.

But for the game to work, the blocks had to vary slightly in size. Slight dissimilarities were inevitable when the bricks were handmade, of different woods, but I feared these random variations would be difficult to mimic when manufactured by machine out of a single kind of wood. Pat came up trumps, devising a sanding template that we could use and suggesting that the bricks could be finished off in a beeswax tumble polisher. This worked like a treat, and in effect, it is still how Jenga bricks are fashioned today.

I then started to look about for a workshop large enough to handle an initial production run of a few hundred games but small enough not to require orders of thousands of units at a time to support it. Another Real Tennis playing friend, Peter Sulston, who worked for Oxfam, suggested that I contact Camphill of Botton Village, Yorkshire, an organization he said he greatly admired.

I had never heard of Camphill, and when invited to visit them to discuss my project, I had no notion of what to expect. What I found was truly amazing. Tucked into a beautiful rugged valley deep in the Yorkshire moors was possibly one of the most unusual villages in England, or so I felt after spending a day there.

My instructions were to drive into the center of the village and turn left past Botton Hall and follow signs to the woodwork shop, where I should park and ask for John Durham. All of which I did, noting as I went the picture-book quality of the village. While I waited for John to arrive, the receptionist offered me a coffee and led me into a side room where there was a display of the wooden toys Botton Hall currently produced. A middle-aged man with the round face, eager manner, and benign smile of a young child accompanied us into the room and stood close by me as I looked at the display.

"Flappy Duck's the best," he declared.

"Is he? Who is Flappy Duck?" I asked.

"He's here. Come," he answered, taking my hand and leading me across the room. "Look!"

The toy he showed me was a wooden duck with leather feet fixed to little wheels at the end of a long pole.

"I'll show you how to do it," he said and enthusiastically pushed the duck-on-a-stick across the floor, causing its leather feet to turn and alternatively slap down on to the tiles, making a satisfying flap-flap-flap-flap noise.

Coming back to where I stood, he stopped and placed my right hand on the pole below his left hand, said, "Like this," and we walked solemnly round the room together pushing the slapping flappy duck before us.

"Ah. I see you have met Tom and been introduced to his favorite toy," I heard a man's voice behind me say. Stopping and letting go of the pole, I turned around to see a dark-haired, pleasantly plump man, smiling and extending his hand

"Hello, I'm John. Welcome."

Shaking his hand, I replied, "Thank you. I'm Leslie. It's lovely to be here. It's a beautiful place."

"Let me show you around the rest of the village before we discuss your game," he said.

Guiding me out of the room, John bade farewell to Tom, reminding him gently to put the toy duck back on the shelf when he was finished taking it for a walk.

On our tour, John explained that Botton Village was a community within the worldwide Camphill Movement, which had been founded in 1940 by Karl König, an Austrian pediatrician and refugee who had worked with children with learning disabilities. König based many of his quite radical beliefs about education on the precepts of the philosopher Rudolf Steiner, who founded the Waldorf School movement.

The Camphill community was home to around 350 people, half of whom had learning difficulties and special needs. The villagers and the co-workers (that is, those people without special needs) lived together as extended families of varying sizes in thirty houses dotted around the village.

John explained that every resident of Camphill's Botton village contributed to the well-being of the community through his or her work, irrespective of ability. Their needs were met, not by a wage system, but by sharing resources according to individual requirements. With no hierarchical management, each resident was encouraged to participate in whatever way he or she could for the good of all.

John went on to describe how the Botton community, although dependent to a degree on financial aid, was able to support itself in large part by farming its own land (650 acres) and running a dairy and bakery, as well as print, glass, and wood workshops.

With justifiable pride, John told me that Botton's wooden toys were now stocked by upmarket toy shops throughout Europe; that Botton supplied many local restaurants and pubs with farm produce, bread, and dairy products; and that Baby Botton, a "small but perfectly formed, cheddar cheese," was even in demand in the food halls of Harrods.

On the way back to the workshop, we stopped off at John's home for a lunch of homemade vegetable soup and fresh bread and perfectly formed, and perfectly delicious, cheddar cheese. John's wife, and I believe most of the members of their extended family (there were nine in all around the table), appeared to play a part in preparing or serving the meal. It was a colorful, joyous, almost boisterous occasion.

After lunch, I showed John my game and told him of Pat's suggestions for creating the handmade effect. We played a quick game, and once again I watched it work its magic. John was hooked and then dismayed when the tower collapsed. Sitting back, he said, "It's great fun. And I think it's unique. I have never played a game that is so intensely competitive yet so cooperative at the same time. You don't want any of your opponents to fail because the tower you are building together will collapse."

He added, "I would be delighted to discuss making the bricks with the team. But I should warn you, because of the nature of our organization, I can't promise that we would be able to handle this work if the game hit the big time and we were expected to produce thousands of sets at a time."

"Would you be prepared for me to order and pay for an initial run with possible repeat orders, knowing that I may have to move on to different contractors in the long run?" I asked.

"I would think so, yes. In fact, it would be the only way we could work. We are a small workshop producing a range of different products. Variety is important to keeping everyone interested in their work, and we would hate to swamp the workshop with just the one product."

This agreed, we moved on to discuss the first order. I had yet to decide how I was going to package the game. I was pursuing a number of different options, so I proposed that in the first instance Botton manufacture and ship to Oxford enough bricks to make up two hundred games, which I would package myself. I had already booked space at the January London Toy Fair to launch the game. John said that he would propose to the team that Botton deliver at least fifty-four hundred bricks, enough for a hundred games, by mid-December, so that I could package and have them ready to show.

My first impression of John was that he was a remarkable man— compassionate, well-balanced, patient, imperturbable, unfailingly good-humored, and fair. On subsequent visits to Botton, throughout the years of what became an increasingly close business relationship, and on the many occasions we met later, usually at trade fairs, my initial impression never altered. Although I have not seen him for some time now, I would wager that he is still the same calm, amiable, and deeply humane person I met in 1982.

While I can't claim to have studied and therefore fully understand anthroposophy, the spiritual philosophy based on the teachings of Rudolf Steiner that underpins the Camphill movement, I will say, having witnessed its practical application at Botton, that anthroposophy has a tremendous, life-affirming appeal—even to a hardened skeptic like myself. An ethos of kindness, of mutual sympathy and respect, of caritas (neighborly and brotherly love), and genuine fellow feeling pervades the village. It's a joyous community that appreciates play and has learned through play but has avoided mistaking real life for a game. Thus, it isn't run with a winner-takes-all mentality that governs the so-called free enterprise culture of life beyond its gates.

I wish more of us could live this way. The world would be a kinder place. And better still, full of flappy ducks.

FIVE

The Name of the Game

After finding a manufacturer for the game, deciding on a name was the next step. As I mentioned previously, up until that time, my family and I had referred to the game as Takoradi Bricks, after the port city in Ghana where we had commissioned the original wooden bricks. I might well have continued to call the game Takoradi, but I felt that this word wouldn't work as a name. I rejected it possibly because it had already been well used to name a place and that place would have no conceptual link with the game to anyone outside my immediate family and circle of friends. I wanted either a word freshly minted, without any existing connotations, or one that in some way conjured up the essence of the game. Nothing sprang readily to mind.

Some days after I had returned from Botton, I drove out to visit my mother. Living in England for the first time in her life, she had bought an old Cotswold Stone house on the edge of a country village ten miles outside Oxford. My thirteen-year-old brother, home from boarding school for the summer holidays, ran out to greet me as I arrived. He was in a state of considerable excitement. He had just been given his first dog, a golden retriever.

"What's her name?" I asked.

"Well, I think the lady who delivered her called her 'Poppy.' It's a little boring, don't you think?"

"She didn't say 'Poppy,' darling," my mother laughed. "She said 'Puppy' in a rather strong Irish accent! The dog doesn't have a name yet. You can call her what you like."

"What about Goldie?" I said.

"Bor—ing," my brother replied.

"Tosca?" I suggested, the opera fresh in my mind from the production I had seen the previous night.

"Naah. Too posh," said my brother.

"How about Lady Di, or, better still, Princess Diana," suggested my mother.

"I don't think so," groaned my brother, rolling his eyes.

"Playful little thing, isn't she?" I said, watching her tumbling about.

"That's it!" my mother cried.

"That's what?" we asked.

"We should call her Chesa," Mother said.

"That's a great name," I said.

"Chesa? What does it mean?" asked my brother.

"It means 'to play.' Have you forgotten all your Swahili?" I replied.

"Probably. Yes. Chesa. Good, though," he said.

"Here, Chesa. Come on, Chesa," he called, patting his thigh.

The puppy came tumbling toward him.

"Wow. It *is* her name. Look how she comes when I call."

Laughing, I turned to my mother. "Mum, that's given me an idea. Why not something Swahili for the name of my game?"

"Why not indeed?"

"What's Swahili for 'tower'?"

"*Mnara.*"

"Not exactly catchy."

"What about 'wood'?"

"*Kuni.*"

"That means 'firewood' doesn't it? Not sure that's quite the right image!"

"Well, *Mbao*, then."

"That's no good, either, nor is *Mti*, 'a tree.' What's tumble?"

"*Gaa-gaa*," replied my Mum.

"The great game of Gaa-gaa? Playing Gaa-gaa? Hmmmm, not sure."

"Then how about *Kjenga*, 'to build'?"

"Hey, that's more like it. Kjenga. Kjenga." I rolled it around on my tongue.

"Or better still, Jenga— the imperative, meaning 'build(!),'" my mother added.

"That's perfect!" I enthused. "That's its name. I'll call it 'Jenga'!" And Jenga it was, Jenga: The Perpetual Challenge.

Although I was attracted to the word *jenga* because of its definition in KiSwahili, I chose to name the game "Jenga" because of the almost palpable feeling of the rightness of the word in English and because I assumed that the word, in English, would *not yet* be a description of anything.

The Magic of a Word

I checked the *Oxford English Dictionary* to reassure myself that *jenga* didn't exist as an English word, but it was just plain luck that it seems not to be recognized as a word in any other language either, aside from KiSwahili. Well, at least if it is, no one has yet pointed this out or attached to it any bizarre or untoward meaning, unlike what happened to Coca-Cola in China. Apparently, when Coca-Cola was first marketed in China, they used the Chinese characters they were told best approximated the sound "co-ca-co-la," which were ke + kou + ke + la. Unfortunately, no one pointed out until much later that the product was simply not selling in China because "ke-kou-ke-la" means "bite the wax tadpole."

So, why did this word *jenga* feel so right to me? Why, when most new words failed, did it succeed? And why, despite this success, have I avoided—albeit unconsciously until now—launching any other game with a seemingly meaningless word for its name?

I'm not sure that there are definitive answers to these questions, but in skimming through the field of linguistics and adding an idea or two from my own experience, I would like to propose a few reasons that seem plausible—at least to me.

In the English language, *jenga* is a neologism, a recently coined word. When a word is no longer new it is, by definition, no longer a neologism. However, opinions differ on exactly just how old, or how frequently used, a word has to be to be considered no longer a neologism. The sad truth is that most poor little neologisms die at birth or in infancy, too weak to ever mature and endure the mysterious initiation rites that seemingly grant entry into full "wordhood" of a language.

It is true that words strong enough to work their way into a language have in the main been assembled from old words or morphemes, the smallest meaningful pieces of a word. Or, as Steven Pinker suggests, the words are "retooled" by applying one or more of a number of devices linguistics scholars have identified as follows: prefixing, suffixing, changing a part of speech, acronyms, truncation, portmanteau, back-formation, metaphor, metonym, and, of course, borrowing. (Pinker is professor of psychology at Harvard University and author of *The Language Instinct* [William Morrow, 1994].)

Nevertheless, creating a new word by using any of these methods does not in itself offer any guarantee of success. The chances of its surviving beyond its conception are still infinitesimally small. There must be other forces at play. To inveigle its way into a lexicon, a word must somehow satisfy all the cognitive and conceptual requirements of a particular language. But what are these requirements?

Well, one of them must be that a word should fill a lexical gap and describe a phenomenon, either for the first time or in an impressive and memorable style. Then, if it is to live on in a language, either the phenomenon it describes has to remain current and continue to require a descriptor, or the word itself has to evolve, gathering nuances, shades of meaning, at each step of the way.

Take *agnostic* as an example, which came about presumably because there arose a need for a word to describe the growing number of people who were neither firm believers nor atheists but who claimed it was impossible to know whether a deity exists or not. In 1869, the English biologist Thomas Henry Huxley came up with this term by compounding the prefix *a* meaning "not" or "without" with the adjective *gnostic*, "relating to knowledge, especially knowledge of spiritual truths." And since there are still plenty of agnostics about, the word has been in use ever since.

Pheromone is another interesting case. Tristram Wyatt, in an essay in *Nature* (January 2009), celebrates the fiftieth anniversary of the word *pheromone*, first proposed by Karlson and Lüscher in a letter in *Nature* (January 1959), to describe the chemical communication between individuals of the same species they believed, but had yet to prove, must exist.

Their timing, Wyatt points out, was perfect: Later that year the first chemical identification of a pheromone, *bombykol,* the sex pheromone of the silk moth, was published, thus demonstrating that chemical signals between animals were actual and could be identified.

Over the intervening years, biologists have identified all manner of ways in which all manner of animals, from ants to elephants, communicate by taste and smell. However, there appear to have been heated discussions as to whether all such chemical signals can be accurately described as pheromones, or more accurately, whether the term *phero-mone* accurately describes each such chemical signal.

Although the complex niceties of what is or isn't a pheromone is a little outside the scope of this book (and, in truth, way beyond my own grasp of the subject), what is fascinating is that the word *pheromone* has stuck. Biologists appear to be willing to tweak or broaden its definition to encompass new meanings rather than ditch it and find a new word.

Pheromone—derived from the Greek *pherein*, "to transfer" and *hormōn*, "to excite or stir up"—remains fit for purpose, and there's apparent life in the fifty-year-old word yet.

While creating a new word to fill a lexical gap may explain why new words are created in the first place and why some go on to survive, it doesn't explain why some phenomena never acquire names. One would have thought that as soon as a cavity was spotted, there would be a rush to plug it, especially when you consider the material we have at our disposal, the hundreds of thousands of meaning-rich morphemes just waiting to be picked for the job. Yet, for some reason, there are gaps in every language that stubbornly refuse to be filled. There is as yet no word for bunting in Swahili, though every time a new shop or gas station is opened around Kenya, its forecourts are festooned with the stuff. *Ana ya vitambaa vya rangi-rangi kwa ajili ya bendera na mapambo (kwenye barabara na majumba wakiti wa sikukuu)* is how bunting is defined by the *Tuki English-Swahili Dictionary*, second edition. Roughly, this translates as "little pieces of cloth of many colors hung as flags and decoration (along the side of roads and on buildings on holidays and festivals)." Bunting, in other words.

And why, when we have so many words of our own, do we English speakers turn to the French when looking for just the right word—*le mot juste*?

And why, in English at least, is there still no satisfactory term for a heterosexual unmarried couple? My *now* husband, Fritz Vollrath, and

I had lived together (for want of a better expression) for ten years and had had two children who were nine and seven years old before we *finally* (my mother's word, not mine) married. And we only married when we did because our lawyer advised us that in English law there was neither a word nor an agreed definition for our state of unwedded *bliss* (my word, not the lawyer's). We were planning to spend prolonged bouts of time in the bush in Kenya and wanted to make sure our wills were in order, our property distributed, and our children cared for in the manner we wanted in the event either or both of us died. The lawyer warned us that there would be screeds of writing and some serious expense involved to bring about the state of affairs we wanted. Such a state, she added with a sigh, would exist by default if we were married, if we would but consent to become husband and wife. So we married for want of the right turn of phrase—because of a lexical gap.

It is conceivable that what we are looking at in this example is not just a gap, but a yawning chasm that it would be impossible to expect a single word or short phrase to fill. Perhaps we cannot find a universally acceptable and legally binding term with the same weight as *marriage* because there is no universally accepted idea of what it means to be an unmarried couple. Perhaps the reason for this is that couples choose to remain unmarried precisely because they have no desire to conform to a universally acceptable idea.

But back to my point. If a lexical gap needs filling and can be filled, will any old word do the job? Specifically, when I designed a new game, and thus created a need for a name, might I have called it anything with similar effect or even any affect? Does the word *jenga* have any intrinsic properties that would have led inevitably to the success of the word as a name of this particular game? Does either the sound of the word spoken or the look of the word written tell us anything about how the word is being used?

For the past hundred or so years, the standard view among traditional language theorists was that, with the exception of onomatopoeia like *crash, bang,* and *wallop,* the relation of a sound of a word to its meaning is entirely arbitrary. This presumably means that I should have been able to string together any combination of sounds to come up with a novel word as a moniker for the game. Yet, having spent a lifetime playing with words while devising word games (Swipe, Anagram, Ex Libris, Bookworm, Inspiration, Flummoxed), naming games, describing games, and considering the resonance of words in one way or another, I intuitively cling to the idea that sounds in themselves should at least hint at the sense of the word they refer to.

But then again, what do I know? It's highly conceivable that, as a Monty Python devotee in my late teens, I was overinfluenced by the ludicrous Woody and Tinny Words sketch. That's the one in which a father, a mother, and a daughter discuss the confidence-inspiring woody quality of words such as *sausage* and the alarming and frighteningly tinny quality of words such as *litterbin.* The sketch ends with the daughter in tears over the awful PVC-ness of the word *leap.*

In fact, long before *Monty Python's Flying Circus's* comic take on life, there were serious scholars of linguistics in the thirties, J. R. Frith, for one (best known today for coining the almost Pythonesque warning, "You shall know a word by the company it keeps.") who suggested that certain sounds might well be associated with certain meanings (a phenomenon Frith called phonaesthesia) even where they do not attempt to imitate a noise (as in onomatopoeia). Frith explained his views in *The Tongues of Men* (Watts & Co., 1937) and *Speech* (Benn's Sixpenny Library, 1930).

An example of a phonaesthetic combination of sounds (a phonoaestheme) may be the *sl* in English words such as *slippery, slick, slide, slither,* and *slime*—with the poor old slug being given its name because of the connotations of the *sl* sound. Perhaps, too, this is why we have immoral women who *slide down slippery slopes* or *slip up* and become *sluts* and *slatterns* and *slags.*

According to Peter Roach (*A Little Encyclopaedia of Phonetics*, available online at www.personal.reading.ac.uk), recent *phonotactic* studies of English have come up with other strange findings: certain sequences seem to be associated with particular feelings or human characteristics, for no obvious reason. Why should *bump, lump, hump, rump, mump(s), clump,* and others all be associated with large blunt shapes? Why should there be a whole family of words ending with the phoneme *le* that all have meanings to do with clumsy, awkward, or difficult action—*muddle, fumble, fiddle, struggle, wriggle, waddle,* and *tumble*? Furthermore, Roach asks, why can't English syllables begin with pw/ bw/ tl/ dl when pl/ bl/ tw/dw are acceptable?

Looking to find an explanation for that tip-of-the-tongue experience we all encounter at some stage, researchers have discovered that the sound of a word can be as important as the meaning of a word when trying to retrieve that word from memory.

It has been suggested by researchers at the University of Texas that "product names with vowel sounds that convey positive attributes about the product are deemed more favorable by consumers" ("Phonetic Symbolism & Brand Name Preference," Tina Lowrey and L. J. Shrum, *Journal of Consumer Research*, October 2007, 406–14). The researchers created fictitious brand names that varied only by one vowel sound (e.g., nillen/nallen). They then varied product categories between small, fast, sharp objects—such as knives or convertibles—and products that are large, slow, and dull, such as hammers and SUVs. They asked participants to choose which of the word pair they thought was a better brand name for the product.

Overwhelmingly, participants preferred words with *i* (as in *Nillan*) sounds when the product category was a knife or a convertible, but they preferred words with *a* (as in *Nallen*) or *u* (as in *Nullen*) vowel sounds when the product category was a hammer or an SUV. The vowel sound "yoo" as in *putrid* is a no-no whatever the product.

So, if you're the kind of person who wants to drive one in the first place, you would rather be seen in a Hummer than a Himmer. And a Humor you would definitely avoid.

When I plucked the word *jenga* from thin air, was I instinctively tuning in to something in the sound of the word that would convey some positive attribute of the game I was about to describe? Maybe so, if you accept Steven Pinker's suggestion that *j* could possibly be considered a sound symbol for *sudden motion.*

To illustrate, he lists *jerk, jab, jagged, jostle, jam, juggle, jiggle, jibe, jangle.* To which I would add *joust* and, of course, *jenga.*

Perhaps more intriguing, in considering the sound of the word *jenga* is that, although it isn't an English word, *jenga* sounds as if it could be. It might contain a sound symbol that conjures up images of sudden motion, but nothing about the word itself grates or jars. It seems to have been assimilated into English without any fuss, which is exceedingly odd if you consider that it doesn't rhyme with or bear any relationship to any other word in the English language, at least not as far as I can tell. Discussing this recently with a friend, a poet, he suggested that the *a* sound at the end of *jenga* gives the word a feminine ending, which balances the more masculine, jabbing *j* at the start, making it a "comfortable" word to use in English.

It may well be "That which we call a rose by any other name would smell as sweet," but would you bother to sniff it, even give it a chance, if another name didn't in some way evoke the beautifully perfumed flower your experience has led you to expect of something currently dubbed rose?

Granted, this is a slightly different question from asking if the sound of the hitherto meaningless word *jenga* might in itself evoke the idea of "game" at all, let alone a hitherto unknown game.

Frankly, I don't think so. I don't think anyone hearing "Jenga" *for the first time* out of context would necessarily think "game," let alone the game it now names. But what I do think is that, having experienced the game and heard its name, you will remember them both *in association* with each other. And this is because there is something about the game Jenga that fulfills our expectation of what a game should be in the first place, and there is something about the word *jenga* that satisfies our idea of what a game might be called.

The linguist and philosopher Ludwig Wittgenstein once famously devised a word game in which he asked his readers to "play" with the word *game*. The point of his game was to show not only that it is impossible to come up with a satisfactory, clear-cut definition of the word but also that, more important, we don't need a precise definition of the word in order to know a game when we see one.

Wittgenstein's game took the form of a thought experiment in which readers are asked first to think of a definition of the word *game*. This, he says, appears simple enough until you consider the problems with each of the possible definitions. Any definition that focuses on amusement leaves us unsatisfied, since the feelings experienced by a world-class chess player are very different from those of a circle of children playing duck-duck-goose. Any definition that focuses on competition will fail to explain the game of catch or the game of solitaire, and a definition of the word *game* that focuses on rules will fall on similar difficulties.

This, he argues, is because there is nothing common to *all* games; rather, games hold certain similarities and relations with each other. Some games involve winning and losing, but not all; some are entertaining, but not all; some require skill or luck, but not all.

He goes on to say, "I can think of no better expression to characterize these similarities than 'family resemblance'; for the various resemblances between members of a family: build, features, color of eyes, gait, temperament, etc., overlap and crisscross in the same way . . ." (*Philosophical Investigations*, Blackwells, 1953, 67).

He adds that although family resemblances might be taken to have "blurred edges," in such cases the term nevertheless has a sense. For example, one can quite sensibly say "stand roughly there," indicating a spot by pointing. The lack of precision does not make the expression meaningless. Similarly, even though any definition of *game* may be imprecise, it is still meaningful. Furthermore, a sharp boundary can be chosen to suit whatever purpose one has to hand. In such cases, it is the way in which the term is employed and how it is learned that are pivotal, rather than any precise meaning.

I would like to extend this concept of "family resemblances" and suggest that one of the reasons why one neologism may make it while another doesn't is because the one that makes it holds traits in common with an existing family of words used to label or define a similar or somehow related concept. We may not be able to pinpoint exactly why, but the word feels somehow familiar.

"We are all, Esme decides, just vessels through which identities pass: we are lent features, gestures, habits, then we hand them on. Nothing is our own. We begin in the world as anagrams of our antecedents" (Maggie O'Farrell, *The Vanishing Act of Esme Lennox*, Harcourt Education, 2006, 134).

This idea that our ancestors' traits are "rearranged" in us appeals to me. Fleetingly, for reasons I can't identify, my daughter can remind me of my grandmother, though she looks much more like her father's mother. A cousin who shares no discernible physical traits with my father will suddenly laugh exactly as I recall my father did.

I wonder: Is it too far-fetched to suggest that Jenga might feel familiar and therefore acceptable because, as an African word, it holds echoes of the distant African past we all share?

Naming products is big business. In the business of naming there are many consultancies that promote themselves as naming specialists, or "naming architects," suggesting that they hold the key to the secret of picking just the right name for a product. Switching metaphors, one (nomen.com) claims to be "well-trained in naming acrobatics."

Scrambling to find the right words to define what it is that they do, expert "namers" like to talk of research, of gathering, and of measuring and evaluating data, all of which implies that naming might be an exact science. But then they rather confusingly suggest that "crafting" a name is an intuitive, creative process that fits more comfortably into the domain of the sensitive artist or wordsmith than the objective and calculating scientist.

To be fair, I think it is entirely understandable that they have problems describing what they do, given that there is no general consensus about how our minds process language in the first place. A poet can dedicate a lifetime to finding just the right word to express a thought, knowing that despite all this effort few people will be able to grasp his meaning.

The truth is that however eloquent and potent the word chosen to name a product might be, a name does not *create* the product or turn something inferior into something great.

In coming up with the name Viagra for Pfizer's male potency drug, Clement Gallaccio (Nomen USA) proved indeed that he has, as he says on his blog, "a knack for recognizing what's a future power brand and what's a mere collection of random letters." Viagra is an ingenious and apposite word, with "vi" suggesting vigor and vitality and "agra" more or less rhyming with *Niagara*, conjuring up an image of a mighty flow. Yet, if there had been no call for the drug or if it had been ineffectual, I suspect that *Viagra* the word would have faded away with the drug.

But, and this is a big BUT, a product can be recognized, distinguished, set apart by its name. An idea can become graspable by its name, and if it's a very strong idea, the idea and its name will live on, inseparable.

Alan Hassenfeld, the chairman of Hasbro, the $4 billion U.S. toy corporation that now produces Jenga, told me, "People might try and copy the game, but the one thing you can't take away from Jenga is its name."

Talking to me about how important it is to him for the company his grandfather and great-uncle started, the original Hassenfeld Brothers, to retain the culture and ethics now embodied in the Hasbro name, Alan said, "You come into this world with nothing, but when you leave it, you leave one thing behind—your name."

I think when I "pointed" at my game and called it "Jenga," I took something that was recognizable as a game and something that was vaguely recognizable as a word and brought them both into sharp focus as though using a pair of binoculars.

I created a bond between the two so that today a particular kind of game is defined by the word *jenga* and Jenga means a particular kind of game. Thus *jenga* will be Jenga as *boys* will be boys and *horse* is a horse, of course. Such is the power of a name.

SIX

Patently Obvious

Before I launched Jenga at the London Toy Fair in January 1983, I made an appointment to see a patent agent to discuss how best to protect the game. However rationally I might now discuss the risks associated with treating business as a game, my instincts as a seasoned games player kicked in the moment I decided to step into business on my own. Assuming that there were rules of engagement peculiar to business, I felt that by taking the game to market I would attract competitors who would consider it fair play to copy the game if I took no steps to prevent that.

The office of Swann, Elt & Co., Patent Attorneys, comprised two very poorly lit, dank, and dingy basement rooms in an otherwise rather swanky Beaumont Street, Oxford, building. In one sat Mr. Jukes the patent lawyer, in the other his secretary. Though I came to know Mr. Jukes well over the next twenty years, and to greatly value his professional advice, I never quite managed to shake off my first impression that I was engaging in some sort of illicit activity, necessitating a shifty look over my shoulder each time I descended Swann, Elt & Co.'s stairs to reveal my latest toy. Adding to the apparently clandestine nature of the encounter, Mr. Jukes would, for reasons I never understood, always proffer his advice in a whisper, having first made certain he had told me, also in a whisper, what his fee for the consultation would be.

On seeing Jenga and having me explain the game, Mr. Jukes whispered that in his opinion it would be worth trying to patent it, though we might encounter some resistance.

"You must understand," he whispered—and I leaned forward in my chair to catch each very expensive word—"that to be granted a patent you must be able to show that your invention employs a novel concept or device. One cannot, for example, patent a new card game. Even though the rules of play may be novel, the device employed—in this case a deck of playing cards—is not novel.

"Now in J— er . . . Jenga, did you say?" I nodded. "You are employing a set of fifty-four wooden blocks that appear at first glance to be a standard set of children's building blocks to play a novel game. But if I understand you correctly, the blocks have had to be carefully engineered to enable the game to work. Each one, while appearing to be the same size as each other one, is in fact slightly, albeit randomly, different in size within set parameters? Yes?" Again I nodded.

"Well, if we word this application with care, I think we might be able to make the case that the game you have devised is, as required by patent law, an innovative step not obvious to those proficient in the art. If you can leave me this set of bricks, I will draw up the application and register it so that you can be allocated a patent-pending number to display clearly on your product's packaging before exhibiting it to the public for the first time. To protect your innovation beyond Great Britain and Northern Ireland, you will be required to apply for a separate patent in each territory in which you seek protection within a year of this, the date of your first registration. This will become exceedingly expensive, I warn you, but you have a year's grace in which to decide if proceeding beyond and spending this money will be worth your while.

"Moving on, there are two more things I strongly recommend. One is to trademark the name *Jenga* and the other is to copyright the rules of the game. Trademarking is done by applying to the UK patent and trademark office for a trademark, which I can do for you, and you can copyright the rules yourself. You just need to include a sentence below the last sentence of any text." He leaned across and carefully wrote out the following on the legal pad he had placed between us: "© copyright Leslie Scott 1982 All rights reserved."

How a Game Becomes a Classic

It might appear that I am contradicting myself in suggesting, as I have done, that Jenga's success was due in part to its *obviousness* while at the same time letting you know that I was able to apply for a patent for the game because, in Mr. Juke's opinion, it was an "innovative step not obvious to those proficient in the art."

Perhaps it would be better to describe the game as "unobtrusive" rather than "obvious"—so unobtrusive that it managed to slip into the canon of classic games with little or no fanfare and nestles there now as though to the manor born

Later in this book, I talk about how Jenga was taken on by Hasbro, and how some of the most able people in the toy business were involved in this process. Recently I had a chance to ask three of these key men, independently, why Jenga had become such a phenomenally successful game.

Alan Hassenfeld said, "First of all, it's simple and it's fun. It takes you no time at all to learn how to play Jenga. It's simple, but it's got everything: frustration, excitement, a precarious situation, and exhilaration. There is a winner and a loser, which is important. And there is the WOW factor when you take that one brick out and the whole thing falls."

Hal Ross, formerly a sales director of Canada's Irwin Toy Ltd., said, "It was different. It was very different, but we couldn't describe why it was different, but it was so simple it was wonderful."

George Irwin, chairman and CEO of Irwin Toy, said, "It was one of those crazy stupid things that come along from time to time, and it worked. In a world that was getting more and more complex, this was something simple and sometimes simple works."

Each of these men is renowned throughout the toy world for an almost magical ability to pick and back a winner. Yet, even they seem unable to pinpoint and articulate what it is about Jenga that explains its success, other than to say that it's simple, and simple in this case worked.

But why did simple work?

Well, I think we like to play games for reasons that are multifaceted and multilayered, some of which I discuss later. I think Jenga is pleasing because it addresses much of what we want from a game, in the simplest way possible. Good design is all about providing the simplest, the most economical, and the most elegant solutions to a problem. However complex the problem, we instinctively prefer the simple solution to the convoluted or complicated.

And yet, not all successful games to have stood the test of time are either as simple as Jenga or appear to have required so little consciously creative input into their design. Monopoly, for example, perennially one of the world's top-selling board games (more than 200 million sets have been sold to date) passed through many design stages, including several changes of name, and had been turned down in 1934 by both Milton Bradley and Parker Brothers for "being too complicated and taking far too long to win to appeal to the masses." Tim Walsh in his book *The Playmakers: Amazing Origins of Timeless Toys* (Keys Publishing, 2004) records that Parker Brothers cited "fifty-two fundamental errors" in the game. Fifty-two? The mind boggles at the idea of being able to identify so many rules of good game design in the first place, let alone recognize when they have been broken.

Ironically, despite their damning analysis, within the year, Parker Brothers had made a complete volte-face, had struck a deal with Charles Darrow (who claimed to be the game's inventor despite the fact that Miss Elizabeth Magie held the original patent), and had published and sold 250,000 games.

In *The Playmakers*, Walsh quotes Phil Orbanes, former head of research and development at Parker Brothers, as suggesting that the reason Monopoly got off to such a phenomenal start in 1935 was that America was in the middle of the Great Depression: "No one had any money and along comes this chance for people to vicariously wheel and deal for a few hours and get their minds off their own personal limitations. When the depression lifted and better economic times followed, people still wanted to fantasize about untold fortunes in paper money (52)."

I think Orbanes reasonably explains why, against all odds and despite its "fifty-two fundamental errors," the game caught on in the 1930s. Why it still sells in such vast numbers today, I would like to suggest, has more to do with a heritage factor than its intrinsic merit as a game or relevance to modern life (well, modern life before the recent Wall Street crash).

Our grandparents suffering through that appalling depression of the thirties—which impacted even the lives of those living in Tanganyika, as in the case of my mother's parents, who had to sell their tea farm for a song and leave their beloved home—very probably did enjoy Monopoly for the reasons Orbanes suggests. Having enjoyed it, they then introduced it to their children who, remembering the enjoyment of playing it with their parents, handed it on to us. And even though I hadn't played the game more than once or twice since playing it with my parents as a child, I, of course, bought a game to play with my own children, who will probably buy one for theirs.

Today there are so many visual and verbal references to Monopoly that whether it is a good game or not seems immaterial, given the iconic role it plays in our culture. It has gone way beyond being susceptible to the vagaries of fashion. If you have any board games in your home at all—and you may be surprised to know that even in this age of the Xbox, Playstation, etc., most families still have a cupboard full of nonelectronic playthings and games—odds are, one of them will be Monopoly.

The French intellectual Roger Caillois, in his 1952 classic work *Man, Play and Games* (University of Illinois Press, 2001), talks of the social function of games and devotes a chapter of his book to looking at how games become a part of our daily lives. He goes as far as to suggest, "Indeed, these manifestations contribute to the development in various cultures of their most characteristic customs and institutions" (41).

Although he is likely to have been thinking more along the lines of national pastimes such as football, cricket, or boules at the time he made this statement, I think it fair enough to add Monopoly to the list, as I believe Monopoly may be considered to have contributed to defining our culture, if only in a comparatively small way.

And Jenga, too? Jenga has certainly become a part of daily life. Can it possibly be lending a little bit of character to our culture? If so, it's for reasons quite different from those driving Monopoly. Jenga, I believe, was taken up because it is simple and obvious—obvious because, in some way, it satisfies some sort of innate understanding we have in our culture of the prerequisites of a game, indeed, of play itself.

The Dutch historian Johan Huizinga, in his seminal work of 1938, *Homo Ludens: A Study of the Play Element in Culture* (Paladin, 1970), argues that play precedes culture: "Play is older than culture, for culture, however inadequately defined, always presupposes human society and animals have not waited for man to teach them their playing. We can safely assert, even, that human civilization has added no essential feature to the general idea of play" (19).

He then goes on to say, "Archaic society plays as the child or animal plays. Such playing contains at the outset all the elements proper to play: order, tension, movement, change, solemnity, rhythm and rapture" (36).

I would advocate that contemporary society still "plays as the child or animal plays" and that, for a game to be adopted and absorbed by a culture and contribute something to that culture, that game must usually contain at the outset all the seven elements Huizinga stipulated as "proper to play." I believe Jenga includes all seven elements if they are defined as follows:

- Order: It has clear and simple rules that the participants are happy to follow.
- Tension: It creates a situation or condition of suspense or uneasiness, even hostility at times.
- Movement: Its play involves physically and skillfully moving blocks from one place to another.
- Change: The "building" changes over time from a stable low structure to a comparatively tall and unstable tower.
- Solemnity: It requires concentration and willingness to take the challenge seriously.
- Rhythm: Players must take turns within a regular and acceptable period of time.
- Rapture: It provides high emotion and intense pleasure. (Just watch and listen to people as the tower begins to teeter and then fall.)

In *Man, Play and Games*, Caillois further states, "There is no doubt that play must be defined as a free and voluntary activity, a source of joy and amusement . . . In effect, play is essentially a separate occupation, carefully isolated from the rest of life and generally is engaged in with precise limits of time and place" (6).

We play from choice. And we choose to play because play allows us to temporarily step away from ordinary life into a world of make-believe. During play, the complicated and confusing laws of ordinary life are, for a brief time, replaced by the straightforward and understandable rules of a game. The rigid structure of play offers a manner of freedom we appear to enjoy—a freedom to experiment, to test ourselves without risk of harmful and permanent repercussions.

Caillois observes that play is governed by rules that for the duration of a game establish new regulations, give all participants an equal chance of winning, and ensure that the outcome is unpredictable. "The game consists of the need to find or continue at once a response which is free within the limits set by the rules" (8).

He goes on to distinguish between the two types of play that he calls, respectively, *Paidia*, "a primary power of improvisation and joy," and *Ludus*, "the taste for gratuitous difficulty." If I understand him correctly, I believe that what Caillois refers to as "Paidia" encompasses three of Huizinga's seven essential elements of play: movement, change, and rapture; and that the "Ludus" he talks of provides three others: order, solemnity, and rhythm. I'm not sure if Huizinga's seventh element, tension, should be categorized as Paidia or Ludus; possibly either or both.

In attempting to find a classification principle that might be applied to the infinite variety of games that exist, Caillois suggests that we consider Paidia at one extreme and Ludus at the other end of a scale of the different types of play. All the games we play might be placed on a continuum between these two poles with, for example, an infant laughing at his rattle located very close to Paidia, and chess positioned at the opposite end toward Ludus.

This scale of Caillois', which includes at least four subdivisions between Paidia and Ludus, has been universally adopted—by computer game enthusiasts in the main—as a means of classifying the complex play value of games. Many discussions take place about where, precisely, along Caillois' scale different games should be placed.

Well aware of the risk in doing so, I am going to stick my neck out and suggest that in Jenga the simple joy of playing with children's blocks is in equilibrium with the gratuitous difficulty of competing against gravity. And this unique and almost perfect balance between Paidia and Ludus might explain the game's universal appeal. It also might explain why Jenga is, quite literally, so patently obvious.

SEVEN

Trademarks and Other Hazards

Though I had applied for a patent for Jenga and had been advised that a full patent was likely to be granted, I was forced to drop my application after the twelve-month patent-pending period because I simply could not afford the crippling fees that were required to proceed in the United Kingdom, let alone any other territory. From 1984 onward, Jenga had to sink or swim without the legal life raft of a patent. I am, therefore, eternally grateful to Mr. Jukes for advising me to trademark Jenga and so protect my rights in this name.

The Bread of Knowledge

Curiously enough, in addition to a patent agent practicing law in the twentieth century, it is a baker of the thirteenth century who must be thanked for the daily crust Jenga earns me today.

Although grain was frequently in short supply, bread had been a staple diet in Britain (and much of Europe) for centuries before a law was passed to regulate bakers. The Assize of Bread (1266) was an attempt to finally fix the size, weight, and price of loaves in relation to the price of wheat. Under this law, only authorized bakers and their employees were allowed to make and sell bread.

The traditional way to register a baker and thus to ensure the provenance of a loaf was the use of a baker's mark, a die made from wood or metal that was stamped on the underside of the bread before baking. Usually simple motifs such as flowers or letters of the alphabet, these marks are believed to be the first trademarks. Registering the mark with the local authorities ensured that a maker could be identified if the loaf was underweight or made of inferior flour. The Judgment of the Pillory was invoked if any baker failed to live up to the mark, and there were heavy penalties for anyone found selling unmarked bread or, worse, passing off their product under another man's name.

This use of marks to establish ownership, aid advertisement, and guarantee quality was adopted by a wide variety of trades, from bell making to brewing, with individual craft guilds governing the use of such marks. One of the earliest court cases involving the improper use of a craft guild's marks occurred in England in 1618 when the manufacturer of high-quality cloth sued a competitor who produced lower-quality cloth under the mark reserved by their guild for top-quality cloth.

It was not until the mid-nineteenth century that people began to think of marks as a type of property. By that time, the marks had become distinctive of an individual trader's goods and so attracted valuable goodwill. Trademark law, as we understand it today, only emerged in the 1870s, establishing the right of an owner to take action in the courts against the infringement of his trademark even when there was no intention to deceive on the part of the infringer.

However, the usefulness of such action was limited by the need for a trader to prove that the mark concerned was in fact capable of distinguishing his goods and that it belonged to him in the first place. Thus, in Britain in 1875, the first across-the-board trademark registration scheme was born to enable all traders or commercial entities to secure claims, via the use of a mark, to an identity in the marketplace.

Although trademarks have long been described as a type of property, it is important to qualify here what is meant by *property*. Unlike most other kinds of property, such as a house, the *value* of a trademark does not lie within the mark itself but in the *intellectual concept*, the information, the reputation, the knowledge embodied in that mark.

The term *intellectual property* (IP) emerged in the late 1960s and, though still hugely controversial, is used increasingly to describe a legal field that refers collectively to abstract properties, including patents, copyrights, and trademarks. Under IP law, the holder of one of these properties has certain exclusive rights to the creative work, commercial symbol, or invention that it covers.

Cory Doctorow, in an article in the *Guardian* ("Intellectual Property Is a Silly Euphemism," February 21, 2008), claims that the term *intellectual property* is a "silly euphemism for *knowledge*—ideas, words, tunes, blueprints, identifiers, secrets, databases." He argues that as a body of knowledge is not and can never be owned like a piece of property, it requires "a legal regime that attempts to address the unique characteristics of knowledge, rather than pretending to be just another set of rules for the governance of property." He accepts that knowledge can be "valuable, precious, expensive" and that the state should regulate our relative interests in thought, but he maintains that the state should confine itself to regulating knowledge rather than attempting to re-create the property system.

I agree. But I would argue that, under the collective term *intellectual property*, legal regimes do exist already that address the unique characteristics of a range of different kinds of knowledge. Whether you consider these regimes "fit for purpose," though, tends rather to depend on which side of the fence you sit on. Designers, inventors, and creators are apt to take a view of these issues different from that of the exploiters and consumers of the products of a creative mind.

Nonetheless, legally, intellectual property falls into a number of different categories:

- A copyright, which may subsist in creative and artistic works (e.g., books, movies, music, paintings, photographs, and software), gives a copyright holder the exclusive right to control reproduction or adaptation of such works.

- A patent may be granted for a new, useful, and nonobvious invention. For a limited period, it gives the patent holder a right to prevent others from practicing the invention without a license from the inventor.

- An industrial design right protects the form of appearance, style, or design of an industrial object (e.g., spare parts, furniture, or textiles).

- A trade secret (sometimes either equated with, or a subset of, *confidential information*) is secret, nonpublic information concerning the commercial practices or proprietary knowledge of a business. Public disclosure of trade secrets is commonly prohibited by contract.

- A trademark is a distinctive sign that is used to distinguish the products or services of different businesses. "The strongest protection is reserved for fanciful marks that are purely the product of imagination and have no logical association with the product" (*Eli Lilly & Co. v. Natural Answers, Inc.* [7th Circ. 2000]). An example, perhaps, is the "fanciful mark" known as "Jenga."

The Protection or Suppression of Ideas

In twenty-six years of designing games, many with the graphic designer Sara Finch, I have had some positive and a few tricky encounters with the individual legal regimes described in that list.

Although most of the games we produced were published through our company, Oxford Games Ltd., Sara and I designed a great number on commission for a wide variety of venerable institutions, including the Bodleian Library, the Ashmolean Museum, the British Museum, the National Gallery, and the Royal Shakespeare Company, to name but a few, and for a number of successful businesses, including British Rail, Burtons Biscuits, Marks and Spencer, Madame Tussaud's, Scholastic Press, and Past Times, a chain of stores and catalogues selling primarily historically inspired gift items.

Of all of these arts institutions and businesses, I would say we had a particularly close—and commercially successful—relationship with the Bodleian Library and Past Times. For the Bodleian we produced The Bodleian Game, Ex Libris, and Bookworm; for Past Times we devised Tabula, The Celtic Knotwork puzzle, Comette, Joust, The Sailor's Knot, Victorian Parlour Games, and many I can't at this moment recall. But there's one I could never forget, and that's the one we named "Hazard," which proved to live up to its name.

In a briefing meeting with John Beale, the founder of Past Times, who always had his inimitable finger on the pulse of upcoming trends, he mentioned that he thought *The Canterbury Tales* would be *the* up-to-the-minute historical topic in the coming year. Canterbury, the city, was about to open its latest tourist attraction, The Canterbury Tales Experience, a kind of Disney-esque ride in which you would be able to feel, hear, and *smell* Chaucer's Britain. Having experienced other such endeavors (e.g., The Jorvic Centre in York, where you can "go back in time" to Viking Britain, and, of course, Oxford's very own trip to the past, in which you're given an authentic whiff of the smell of medieval students), I could conjure up an olde worlde image of what was involved. Sara and I, aka Oxford Games, agreed to work on the project.

Reading through my school edition of Geoffrey Chaucer's *The Canterbury Tales* I came across the mention in "The Pardoner's Tale" of a dice game, the name of which was "hazard," which the pilgrims played from time to time along their route.

> In Flaunders whilom was a compaignye
>
> Of yonge folk, that haunteden folye,
>
> As riot, *hasard*, stywes, and tavernes
>
> Wher as with harpes, lutes and gyternes
>
> They daunce and pleyen at <u>dees</u>, bothe day and nyght.

Reading this passage sparked the idea to construct our game around the medieval game of hazard. Players would take a journey from London to Canterbury winning or "collecting" tales as they moved along by playing the game. (It's a little difficult to explain the game without illustrating it, but I hope you get the gist.) The game would consist of a board representing the journey, cards representing the tales, dice, and a booklet with a précis in Modern English of each of the medieval tales.

Past Times approved the idea, the design, and the name "Hazard: A Game of the Canterbury Tales," and by the end of the year we had published the game and it was on sale through the Past Times shops and mail-order catalogues. After several months Oxford Games and Past Times both received a cease-and-desist letter from a patent lawyer on behalf of his client who owned the trademark "Hazard," which he had registered in respect of Class 28 goods, defined by the government patent and trademark office as including "games and playthings, gymnastic and sporting articles not included in other classes, and decorations for Christmas trees."

The letter also stated that the registration gave his client a statutory monopoly on the use of the trademark "Hazard" in relation to the goods and services to which it was registered, and his client would now be seeking damages from us for violating and diluting his mark by publishing and selling our game.

Sara and I were pretty startled to receive the letter; the people at Past Times were considerably less so. It turned out that they received and sent out similar letters on a regular basis. John advised me to acquaint myself with the background of this particular story and then contact his patent lawyer for advice. Meanwhile, we would continue to produce and they would continue to sell our game.

I discovered that the lawyer's client, Mr. H., had devised a board game based on golf, which he had called "Hazard." He had then, apparently, exhibited a prototype of the game at the previous year's London Toy Show. The patent lawyer had approached Mr. H. and convinced him that he should protect his idea by registering the word *hazard* as a trademark. That the lawyer succeeded in acquiring a registered trademark for this word must, in truth, have been as much of a surprise to him as it was to me.

He must have known, as I did, that to be allowed to register one in the first place, a trademark must be distinctive and "not descriptive of the nature or purpose of the goods or services for which the registration is sought," as is made clear in a pamphlet issued by the UK Patent and Trademark Office.

You can't, for example, register "chair" as a trademark for a seat with a back that usually has four legs and sometimes arms.

Similarly, you can't register "chess" as a trademark for a game of skill played by two persons, each of whom moves pieces on a checkerboard according to fixed rules.

Nor, in my opinion, should you be able to register the word *hazard* as a trademark for a game when the dictionary's first definition of the word is "a game of dice in which the chances are complicated by a number of arbitrary rules" (*The Compact Edition of the Oxford English Dictionary*, 1971) and when all other meanings of the word *hazard* derive from its first meaning as *this particular* game of chance or risk.

Even the hazards in golf—obstacles such as bunkers, roughs, or water—are so called because of the word's original denotation as the game of chance that was said by William of Tyre, the twelfth-century chronicler of the Crusades, to have been invented during the siege of the castle of Hasart or Asart in Palestine. John Wycliffe mentions the dice game circa 1380: "And fallen to nyse pleies at table chess and hasard" (*The English Works of Wyclif Hitherto Unprinted*, Adamant Media Corporation, n.d., 151), and the Pardoner hotly defends the playing of the game in Chaucer's *Canterbury Tales*: "Now will I yow deffenden hasardrye."

Hazard, the slippery little word, somehow managed to dodge reviewers in the trademark registration department of the Patent and Trademark Office. Clearly, when considering the word, they failed to pick up a dictionary, encyclopedia, or indeed any book describing the history of games to check if the word *hazard* was "descriptive of the nature or purpose of the goods (services) for which registration is sought." And clearly no similar trademark owner opposed it during the three months it was advertised in the *Trade Mark Journal*.

When I first raised the issue with John's patent lawyer and filled in the background to our game of Hazard, he was gung-ho for us to stand firm and challenge the validity of Mr. H.'s trademark and therefore his right to stop us selling our game. But tens of thousands of pounds of lawyer's fees later I received a phone call from John suggesting we withdraw from this fight and take our game off the market. Revenue from the sales of the game simply did not justify an expensive battle, even though we were very likely to win.

The onus of proof of the validity of a trademark lies with the registered owner of the mark, and a credit check on Mr. H. had revealed that he was unlikely to be able to afford to defend his rights to an exclusive use of this mark. However, John felt—and I agreed—that if anyone was "at fault" in this case, it was the Patent and Trademark Office for granting the mark. As the office could not be held accountable, the only people to benefit from continuing with this matter would be the lawyers. So we took the game off the market, without even going to court. It was the economically sensible thing to do, but it still gets my goat, chiefly because I had put considerable time and effort into researching our game and Hazard the golf game never went into production, as far as I know.

This taught us the expensive yet invaluable lesson to always check to find out if a word had been granted a trademark before using it as the name of a product. Even though "the 'fair use' defense, in essence, forbids a trademark registrant to appropriate a descriptive term for his exclusive use and so prevent others from accurately describing a characteristic of their goods" (*Soweco, Inc. v. Shell Oil Co.* [5th Circ. 1980]), if a word has been registered as a trademark, we knew it was advisable to avoid that word.

We also came to realize that, although the Patent and Trademark Office (today known as the Intellectual Property Office) might be responsible for filing and granting trademarks and patents, and will charge considerable fees for doing so, it is not responsible for defending any intellectual property from infringement.

Cultural Heritage

As I've mentioned, I dropped my application for a patent for Jenga because I simply could not afford the fees I would have had to pay to continue it. However, even if I had scraped enough money together to keep the patent alive in the UK and register it in other regions, I would never have been able to afford to challenge any infringements of the rights I owned in that patent.

It is this particularity of patent law that so agitated James Dyson, the British inventor of the bagless vacuum cleaner, that twice he took a case to the European Court of Human Rights. Yet he lost both times. His argument was that it was illegal and an infringement of a human right that an inventor has first to pay to patent an invention and then has to keep paying to keep the patent registered, whereas an artist or an author owns the copyright to a work of art by default. Worse still, he argued, despite the legal process and the substantial fees involved, the patent that an inventor owns on an invention does not automatically provide protection from having someone copy that invention. For, in court, the onus is still on the patentee to prove his or her inventiveness when accusing someone of copying an invention. Owning a patent is not proof enough of originality, it appears, even though it will only have been granted after a detailed process of inspection and analysis.

Dyson points out that copyright *automatically* protects original creative or artistic works—literature, drama, music, art, layouts, recordings, and broadcasts. The creator of an original work is considered its author and first owner, and in most cases a copyright will last for the life of the work's creator plus seventy years after his or her death. During this period, permission to use copyright-protected material may be required from the copyright holder who may no longer be the original author. A copyright, like any other piece of property, can be sold or given away.

Precisely *what* a copyrightable work of art *is* was amusingly challenged by the American conceptual artist Jonathon Keats (1971–) when in 2003 he copyrighted his mind. Though copyright does not protect ideas for a work unless those ideas are fixed—for example, in writing (and it does not protect the spoken word unless recorded)— Keats argued that it was legitimate to copyright his mind because it could be considered a sculpture that he had created, by neural connections, through the act of thinking. He told the BBC World Service when interviewed about the project that he would attain temporary immortality, on the grounds that the Copyright Act would give him intellectual property rights on his mind for a period of seventy years after his death. He reasoned that, if he licensed out those rights, he would fulfill the *cogito, ergo sum* argument ("I think, therefore I am"), paradoxically surviving himself by seven decades. In order to fund the posthumous marketing of intellectual property rights to his mind, he sold futures contracts on his brain in an "intellectual property office" at the Modernism Gallery in San Francisco.

When we devised and published Ex Libris: The Game of First Lines and Last Words for the Bodleian and the British libraries, Sara and I had a number of interesting encounters with copyright. As we say in the blurb on the back of the box

> Ex Libris is a game to challenge your literary acumen and test your writing skills. Each card gives you the title, author and plot summary of a novel or short story on one side of the card. At the start of a round, one player, taking a turn as the reader, picks a card and reads it out. The other players have to write a plausible opening or closing sentence to the work in an attempt to bluff fellow players into believing their "script" to be the genuine one. These are all handed into the reader, who has meanwhile written down the genuine sentence (given on the back of the card). The winning player is the one who has most votes cast for his or her entry (while further points are won if you manage to identify the genuine sentence). One hundred authors representing widely different writing styles are featured in the game from Charles Dickens to Harold Robbins, from Jane Austen to Barbara Cartland.

At that time (1991), copyright lasted for just fifty years beyond the life of an author. Nevertheless, a large portion of the works we wanted to include in the game still fell within copyright and we needed to seek permission from either the author or the beneficiaries of the author's estate. Where authors were extant, we generally wrote to their agents for permission to quote the first and last lines from a work, explaining that the Bodleian and British libraries were to receive royalties from the sale of the game. In most cases we received favorable replies granting consent without onerous conditions.

For example, Barbara Cartland, the queen of romantic fiction and Princess Diana's step-grandmother, stipulated that she was delighted for us to use her work in return for which she would be *thrilled* to receive a copy of the game once it was published. We sent her a hand-written thank-you note and two copies of the game hot off the press and wrapped in bright pink tissue paper, fluffy pink things being Miss Cartland's trademark.

Late one Sunday evening I received a phone call at home from a Jack Higgins, whose name I couldn't place until he said, "I have your letter requesting permission to quote from *The Eagle Has Landed*. I'm flying out of the country tomorrow morning and thought it easier to ring you than write a letter. You see, I hate writing. Anyway, I just wanted to say, 'Yes, go ahead; fine by me.' People are forever plagiarizing my work, so why shouldn't you? At least you had the courtesy to ask!"

When anyone demanded payment—there were very few who did—we quietly dropped that author and book from the game, usually without much regret. However, in the case of Agatha Christie (1890–1976), excluding her work from the game was a tough call. Not that we had much choice. Agatha Christie Ltd., a company she had set up herself in 1955, refused us permission to use any of her work. Period. No amount of pleading our case had any effect. The company, headed up by Christie's grandson, Mathew Prichard, fiercely and profitably (it earned $5 million in royalties in 1990 alone), guards the intellectual property rights it owns to Agatha Christie's body of work.

Given that Ms. Christie once described herself as "a sausage machine" and confessed that she wrote "exclusively for money," she would in all likelihood have approved of her grandson's mercantile and unsentimental defense of her literary legacy, perhaps even more so his decision in 1998 to sell 64 percent of Agatha Christie Ltd. to Chorion, "an entertainment content" company.

The economist and journalist Victor Keegan suggests that a discussion about the nature of copyright is long overdue ("Why piracy isn't such a bad thing for music," *Guardian*, March 27, 2008). His particular bugbear is the music industry, which he claims has a "misbegotten attitude" to what should be the proper balance between the interests of consumers and those of "corporate lobbyists" who have succeeded in extending copyright in the United States to a "ludicrous" seventy years after the death of the creator—something he says is wrongly "capitalizing on the work of the long-dead." Keegan goes on to say that objective studies (though he does not specify from whose perspective these studies may be considered objective) of the economic consequences have found that a period of fourteen or fifteen years would balance the rights of owners against the economic benefits of allowing other creative artists to rework existing copyrights. Patents, he says, now have a limit of twenty years, which gives the corporation that paid to do the work and patent it the time to make a decent return while enabling them to prepare to exploit the patents of their rivals when they expire—to the benefit of consumers.

Especially in the light of the rise of plagiarism on the Internet, views on this issue are often polarized, ranging from people who believe that the best way to nurture creativity is to support laws that protect people's creations, to those who reject outright the very concept that ideas and creativity should be owned or regulated at all. I find myself plonk in the middle of this debate, yo-yoing from one pole to the other depending on the particularities of a given case.

On the one hand, I feel wholly justified in wanting to protect *my* rights to own and benefit financially from any property I have purchased (my home) or created (my games) for at least as long as I am alive. Both were acquired as a result of my own labor and a willingness to take risks. And, despite what I consider my leftish leanings, I think the heirs to my estate, my husband and children, should be allowed to inherit and benefit from all my property—intellectual or otherwise.

Yet, on the other one hand, I confess to being irritated when I could not include a quintessential English author's work in a game supported by the British Library, which was, in a sense, an anthology of quintessential English writing, just because of the hard-nosed commercial stance taken by the copyright owner. And I was equally, if irrationally, annoyed when I found out that to be allowed to quote from *Winnie the Pooh*, in Bookworm, a children's game we produced for Oxford's Bodleian Library, I had to seek permission from that most American of American companies, the Disney Corporation. Interestingly, unlike Agatha Christie Ltd., they graciously granted permission—and without charge. It surprised me to discover later that Disney had bought the rights to *Winnie the Pooh* in 1961, less than ten years after A. A. Milne died; thus Pooh was technically already an American national when I, as a child, adored him for being *so* essentially *English*.

The language we speak, the jokes we enjoy, the literature we write and read, the buildings we design and live in, the sports we play and watch, the artwork we produce and hang, the films we make and enjoy, the food we cook and eat all play as large a part in defining what it means to be British or American or French or Kenyan as do the physical landscape, the climate, and the history of our native country.

I may have been born and raised in Africa, but as a citizen of Great Britain, I consider myself British. I speak English; I understand rugby and cricket (well, better than I do football and baseball); I studied Shakespeare, Dickens, and Trollope at school; I know the fate, in order, of the six wives of Henry VIII (divorced, beheaded, died, divorced, beheaded, survived); my father was a Spitfire pilot in the Royal Air Force; I genuinely love Marmite; and just like British children everywhere, I grew up reading *Alice's Adventures in Wonderland*, *Peter Pan*, *The Wind in the Willows*, *The Famous Five*, and *Winnie the Pooh*, of course, which, moreover, I consider as integral a part of my culture as cheddar cheese, the Union Jack, and Big Ben. This may seem odd, given that I had no direct experience of Great Britain before I was ten years old and did not leave Africa to make my home in England until I was twenty. Although I also read *Little Women, Little House on the Prairie,* and Superman and Archie comics (in secret—my mother considered comics dreadful rags), I was fully aware that these were *American* stories that gave a glimpse of a culture very different from my own—a culture I confess I sorely envied as a child because *they,* that is, those lucky American kids, had access to such marvels as X-ray specs and Sea Monkeys, wonders I could only dream about owning.

It has been interesting to discover in the course of researching this book that I am not at all alone in holding rather confused and contradictory views about the role of copyright. In fact, according to Lyman Ray Patterson, the author of *Copyright in Historical Perspective* (Vanderbilt University Press, 1968), the way copyright laws evolved made such confusion inevitable, because, he says, there are no clearly defined principles behind the legal concept of copyright. That's why copyright today consists primarily of a series of fragmented rules that seem ill-equipped to resolve the fundamental problems of reconciling the interests—conflicting in some respects, compatible in others—of the author, who conceives and gives expression to ideas, the publisher, who disseminates the author's ideas, and society, which uses these ideas.

Soon after the introduction of the printing press into England by William Caxton in 1476, the government of the day, wishing to keep a tight lid on the spread of seditious ideas, limited the rights to publish work to members of the Guild of Stationers. Essentially, guild members acted as the government's censorship policemen, in return for which service they were granted a monopoly in the book trade, an arrangement that was to last for several hundred years.

With the demise of censorship and no longer supported by governmental sanctions, such copyright law as existed failed to continue to protect the guild's monopoly in published works. Fearing this would mean a total collapse of their businesses, publishers lobbied hard. They insisted that it was in the author's and therefore the public's interest that copyright laws be restored. They argued that without effective laws to protect authors' work against plagiarism and piracy, there would be little incentive for authors to express their ideas and go to print; consequently, society would be denied ready access to ideas.

As a result, copyright laws were reintroduced, this time in the form of a statute, the Statute of Anne. However, because this was designed to promote creativity, education, and learning—as publishers had advocated it should—the protection it offered was for authors, not publishers. It was even then limited to a mere fourteen years from the date of publication. This was not quite what the publishers had had in mind. Hoping for a return to the good old days when they had enjoyed a government-granted monopoly, they had assumed that any new copyright law would inevitably protect their interests, in perpetuity. This statute certainly did not do that. Neither did it result in improving the legal rights of the author, despite the fact that this had been the lawmakers' intention. On the contrary, what had from time immemorial been considered an author's moral right to demand "fair and accurate copy of his or her work *in perpetuity*" was severely curtailed by this statute to just fourteen years.

Nevertheless, one positive outcome of the Statute of Anne was, as the American academic Lawrence Lessig states in an interview on the Massive Change project forum (www.massivechange.com, January 20, 2004), "For the first time in English history the works of Shakespeare, for example, were no longer under the control of monopoly publishers. Works became free and the tradition of free culture was really born." Everyone had the freedom to build *without seeking permission* upon what had been created in the past.

Over the intervening years, through judicious lobbying, publishers slowly inched their way back to a position of control. They did so to a point, some would argue, where today there is a real danger that in a legitimate or at least understandable bid to maximize return on an investment in a piece of work (e.g., a book or film or song), copyright laws are once again being used by publishers to limit society's access to ideas and knowledge—in some cases to its own cultural heritage.

In the same Massive Change interview, Lessig points an accusatory finger at the Walt Disney Corporation, whose founder happily and lucratively created much of his greatest work by building on ideas in the public domain, such as *Grimm's Fairy Tales*. Yet, the corporation has since very successfully persuaded governments to extend copyright, with the effect that an exceedingly long time has to pass before anybody will be free to build on any work the corporation has created or acquired. For example, *Winnie the Pooh* won't be released for many more decades to come.

Today, increasingly desperate to secure the future of the publishing industry, which has been thrown into jeopardy by modern recording, broadcasting, copying technology, and the rise of the Internet, copyright regulations are becoming ever more stringent. In adopting such an extreme vision of copyright protection, we are, according to Lessig, at risk of destroying the very opportunities for creativity and freedom of expression that copyright was originally intended to enable.

At one end of the spectrum we have the All Rights Reserved camp and at the other end we have the No Rights Reserved camp, each claiming its way is the only way of ensuring that creators will continue to create. A fierce debate rages with lawyers such as Lessig, who argues the need for a middle way (i.e., something that enables artists to share work and be fairly compensated for their creativity). If we don't find it, we might well strangle creativity and freedom of expression with ever more contorted rules.

I agree that getting this right is very important, although I have my doubts about whether it would ever be possible to come up with a compromise that would satisfy all parties—designers, publishers, and end users.

Realistically, too, I am not sure that one can (or should) want to escape from having to weigh the risks of developing an idea against possible future rewards. Even those unmotivated by financial gain (fine artists or pure scientists, for example) need some yardstick by which to evaluate their own work, if only on their own terms. This is very difficult to do if there is no challenge or risk involved.

Nonetheless, it could be argued that there are risks enough associated with taking a new product to market (from investing ingenuity, time, and money on developing an idea) to deter all but the very determined, without the added burden of the risk of intellectual-property theft. If we accept the concept of ownership of ideas, I think we should accept the concept of being able to insure or otherwise protect those ideas against infringement and theft, and at a reasonable cost. Even so, in many cases it isn't possible to balance potential loss against the actual expense of protecting work because insurance premiums and "protection money" have to be paid (to the Intellectual Property Office) at a very early stage of development, long before it's feasible to accurately assess the potential market for an idea, and therefore its potential value.

As I have said, I dropped my application for a patent for Jenga when I ran out of funds, but I was lucky. Because Jenga is a game (not a vacuum cleaner or other mechanical device), I was able to copyright the rules of play and so protect the essence of the idea behind the game, and I was able to trademark my "fanciful" name. Thus, in the long run, I was able to generate enough legal and market protection for Jenga to enable me—and many others—to enjoy the benefits of my initial creative and chancy investment.

EIGHT

Taking Jenga to America

In the summer of 1983 I decided I would take Jenga to America. My older brother, Graham, was by then a medical doctor, married, and living and working as an intern at a hospital in Lexington, Kentucky. He and his American wife agreed to act as my agents in the United States. So, with an enormously heavy box containing fifty sets of Jenga, I set off to conquer the United States, hoping for a little more financial success than I had so far achieved in the United Kingdom.

My first stop was New York, where I stayed with a friend, David Morgan, an employee of the Standard Chartered Bank, headquartered in London, who lived in a rather chic tenth-floor apartment in Manhattan. David's sister, Judith, is a very close friend from school days and, although I had known David for donkey's years, I think it pretty likely he had agreed to put me up only under the weight of a little sibling pressure. When he saw me backing out of the elevator dragging an enormous box, he must have sorely regretted capitulating to his sister's demands.

"What the hell have you got in here—" David gasped as we struggled with my luggage, "bricks?"

"Yes, precisely." We staggered into the flat and dropped the box with a thud that shook the room.

"Well," David said looking a little flushed and put out. "Welcome to Manhattan."

"Ahh!" I groaned, sitting on the box. "Thank you, and sorry."

"Would it be too inquisitive of me to ask why you have dragged a box of bricks across the Atlantic?"

"They're not just ordinary bricks. They are the wooden bricks of a game I devised."

"Is that the game I played with you when I visited you and Judith in Oxford? I don't remember it requiring so many bricks."

"One game doesn't, of course. I have fifty games in this box. I have gone into production of the game and have put it on the market under the name of 'Jenga.'"

"I see. Would you like a cup of tea, or a gin and tonic?"

David very graciously allowed me and my bricks to spend the night in his apartment and even to leave the bulk of the games with him when I departed in the morning for my next port of call—Fishers Island in the eastern end of Long Island Sound.

Tolly and Rosie Taylor, an American couple who were good friends from Oxford, where Tolly was studying for a PhD *and* played Real Tennis, spent much of June and July each year at Rosie's family summer home on Fishers Island. I had spent a week with them there the previous year and had fallen in love with this beautiful, understated summer retreat of the seriously wealthy New Yorker. When she heard I would be in New York, Rosie invited me to stay and to bring copies of Jenga, which she thought might prove a hit on the island. Taking a half dozen games with me, I traveled on the Boston-bound train from Grand Central Station to New London, Connecticut, where I disembarked and caught the tiny island ferry to make the forty-five-minute trip across Long Island Sound to Fishers.

Various members of Rosie's extensive immediate and extended family were staying on the property, which comprised a large, rambling Dutch-gabled white-shingle house and a smaller, modern glass-and-wood cottage. Rosie's sisters and brother and several cousins filled the big house, so I joined Tolly and Rosie down the garden in the cottage that was just a hop and a skip from a sheltered and almost entirely private little bay. For the duration of my stay, I slipped effortlessly into the established rhythm of their day. Tolly spent every morning writing an academic treatise on linguistic theory and language development. Rosie pottered about (literally—she made pots). I taught myself to windsurf on a borrowed board by doggedly plowing up and down the little bay. By the end of the week, I had learned how to stay upright and could even come about, though I would have won few prizes for the style in which I executed this particular maneuver.

The evenings were spent in true country house style, eating, drinking, and playing a variety of games, one of which was, of course, Jenga, which everyone appeared to enjoy. Rosie's younger brother, Billy, took a particular shine to it. He loved the game and he liked its association with Camphill, an organization he knew very well, having lived and worked in a Camphill village in Switzerland and another in the United States. He offered to become my "Fishers Island Rep" and took the game to the only gift store on the island, The Gold and Silver Store, coming back triumphantly with an order for a dozen units.

Heading South

Relieved to be returning to Manhattan without all the games I had taken with me, I arrived back at David's apartment. There I spent a second night before dragging my box—now lighter by fifteen games—onto a flight to Lexington, Kentucky, to stay with my brother. Apart from meeting my newborn niece, my plan in Kentucky was to register "Leslie Scott Associates" as a business and open the necessary bank account. After this, I planned to place an ad for Jenga in the *Smithsonian* and *The New Yorker* magazines and begin to sell the game directly to the end user by mail order. My principal goal was to be ready for business once the orders for Jenga came flooding in, as I was convinced they would once I had placed those eye-wateringly expensive magazine advertisements.

My sister-in-law had set up an appointment for me with a so-called new customer liaison officer at the bank where she and my brother held their accounts. I arrived a few minutes before the scheduled meeting time. Miss Juliet, a plump, pretty, well-groomed woman in her early fifties, was seated behind a desk in the open-plan office of the bank. She rose to greet me as I was introduced.

"It's so nice to meet you Mizz Lez-er-lee. Please take a seat. What may I do for you today?" Miss Juliet asked, drawing out the sentence in a slow Kentucky accent and pronouncing *day* as "day-ee."

"I am setting up a business and I would like to open a business account, if I may," I replied.

"Why, of course. We would be delighted to open an account for you. Now, would that be a savings or a checking account?"

"A checking account in the first instance," I said, adding with a hopeful little laugh, "and perhaps a savings account in the not-too-distant future if the business is a success."

"Why, I'm sure it will be a huge success in no time at all."

As she had neither seen the game nor even asked what my business was, I was a little puzzled about what made her so confident. But I let it ride, and sipped the deliciously cool lemonade I had been given while she pulled out a raft of forms from a filing cabinet by her desk and set them before her.

"Before we get too far along in this process, I just want to check that you are able to accept funds from and transfer funds to the UK," I said.

"Oh, absolutely. Why, a good many of our clients have money going in and out of the UK on a regular basis without any problem at all."

Happy that this was not to present a stumbling block, I answered all her questions: What address did I want to use? How many checks did I need in my first checkbook? Was I to be the only signatory on the account?

It was a long, drawn-out affair, but I was not in a hurry, and I was rather enjoying listening to her slow, melodic voice.

Finally, putting her pen down, she looked up and said, "There now. I think that's everything. I must say, Mizz Leslie. I do love your wonderful accent. I've been trying to place it all along. Are you from Ing-ger-land by any chance?"

"Yes. Yes I am," I replied, wondering why, given my question about moving funds from the United Kingdom, it had taken such a long time to conclude that I was English.

"Uh-ha. I thought so. That's so wonderful. I love your royal family." There was a pause.

"Ahh! Well, now. Is there anything else you need to know before I let you go today?"

"I guess, only to ask when the account will be open so I can make arrangements for my UK bank to send funds to you. I assume you will have no problem if they wire the money in pounds sterling for you to convert to U.S. dollars?"

"Why ever would you want to send your money to us in pounds sterling?"

"Because I am sending it to your bank from the UK, where I keep it in sterling pounds."

"You do? May I ask why?"

"Why what?"

"Well, why do you keep it in sterling?"

I was beginning to wonder if Miss Juliet was not just slow of speech but a little slow altogether.

"Well," I said, slowly, "the pound sterling is the currency we use in the UK."

"It is? Ma'am, we have many, many clients at the University of Kentucky, and I had no idea they used the pound sterling."

"The University of Kentucky? Is that what you thought I meant when I said UK?"

"Why, yes'm. What other UK is there?"

"I meant the United Kingdom. You know, Great Britain, England, Scotland, and Northern Ireland?"

"Oh. You want to send money from England?"

"Yes. England. Will that be a problem?"

"Oh, yes. I'm afraid that would be, ma'am. We don't deal with anyone outside of the state of Kentucky. Actually, we don't deal much with anyone outside the city of Lexington, if truth be told."

"In which case, there is little point in me having an account with you."

"Oh, I can see that now, ma'am, and I agree," she replied with disconcerting candor.

"Right, then. Okay, thank you for your time," I said tersely, getting up to leave.

"You are very welcome. It's been a real pleasure. You'all come back and visit soon," she replied, smiling broadly and without a hint of sarcasm in her voice.

Following this somewhat disappointing encounter, I discovered that there were in fact very few international, interstate, or even *inter-county* banks in the United States at that time. Dating back to the Great Depression, when a third of all banks failed, many states had laws in place to restrict banks from branching outside their own home counties. By 1983, these restrictions were beginning to ease, but unlike banks in Britain (e.g., Barclays, Lloyds, etc.) that had a branch on every high street across the country, the banks in the States were still very parochial. Today, after the recent financial crash, I imagine there may be many people who wish this easement of restrictions had never taken place.

I rang David in New York for his advice on how to find the type of bank I needed. He offered to open an account for me in the Standard Chartered Bank's New York branch, which, as a foreign bank, could offer all the facilities I needed. I was exceedingly grateful. I knew he was taking a bit of a risk by waiving the bank's usual prerequisite for accepting a new client—that is, the client actually having some funds to deposit. I had very little. I opened the account by depositing $195.

A Surprising Connection

I don't remember now how I happened to have this odd $195 to spare, but I have a vivid recollection of something else odd that happened to me on the day I deposited that money. The Real Tennis professional Lochlan Duchar was an old friend. Though an Australian, he had worked in Oxford and at Hampton Court Palace and now had a temporary job as the professional at the New York Racquet and Tennis Club. Lochie had suggested that I should contact him if I had time when I was in Manhattan. Coming out of the Standard Chartered Bank's office on Park Avenue, it occurred to me that I was just a block or two from the club and I should seize the opportunity to drop in and say hello.

As I stepped into the revolving door of this beautiful early twentieth-century building, all the more outstanding for being merely five stories high, it struck me once again just what a privilege it was to be associated with this exceptional game. However, I had barely swung into the club's majestic lobby when I found myself unceremoniously pushed, by a large liveried doorman, through the still rotating door and back out onto the street. Sounding anything but apologetic, the man said, "Sorry, ma'am. Persons of the female gender are not allowed into the New York Racquet and Tennis Club." And with no further ado, he swooshed himself back into the club, leaving me standing startled outside.

I was astonished. It had never occurred to me that in 1983, in liberal, tolerant New York, New York, anyone would consider that playing this ancient game entitled him to have his doorkeeper physically eject a woman from the court. Henry VIII would have approved. And, come to think of it, perhaps I had had a lucky escape. I did, after all, manage to keep my head.

Putting this awkward affair out of mind, I set off for the airport and took a flight to Los Angeles, where I had arranged to stay with the family of Gill Grebler, a close friend of mine in Oxford and another one of my doctoral student friends. I had no particular agenda in mind, just a desire to catch up with Gill's parents and sisters, whom I had met on a number of occasions when they had visited Gill in Oxford. Still, I did hope also to secure some new possible outlets for Jenga.

Socially, it was a wonderful visit; from a business point of view, not especially significant—or so I thought at the time. With hindsight, however, I have come to recognize that my visit to the Grebler family in 1983 was the critical first episode in the story of how a business called Pokonobe Associates acquired and still retains ownership of Jenga, and how it came about that Pokonobe Associates, not I as Jenga's author, now assigns and controls the rights to publish my game.

It is a complex story I want to recount in some detail here. Only in the course of recently piecing together and now presenting, in chronological order, details I discovered from sifting through my old contracts, diaries, and correspondence, have I finally begun to understand how, by failing to watch my step, I tripped up and allowed the rights and ownership of Jenga to slip away from me. And although unique to Jenga and me, I believe that my story highlights lessons that will be useful to any creative person engaged in the process of taking an idea to market. It also may explain why, at this stage, I have come to appreciate the importance of asserting loudly my right to be clearly identified as the author—the *only* author—of Jenga.

The First Step

On my visit to California in 1983, I had given Jenga to Gill's parents as a parting gift. Some months later, Gill's brother Robert, visiting his family from Canada, was shown and played this particular game of Jenga. Later still, some time toward the end of 1984, Robert picked up the phone and rang me.

Though I may have forgotten the precise words we exchanged on that day, twenty-five years later I still recall our conversation in some detail. I was surprised but delighted to receive a call from Gill's brother, the only member of her immediate family I had yet to meet. After introducing himself and apologizing for bothering me, Robert told me that he was ringing from Montreal, where he lived and where he owned and managed an oil business. I remember being extremely impressed. My father had worked in the oil business most of his life, I had met oilmen of all shapes and sizes, but I had never, up until that moment, met anyone who *owned* an oil company. I must have said something silly to this effect, as I recall Robert's rather curt reply explaining that these were edible vegetable and nut oils he was importing and distributing. The oil was not the black sticky stuff that's refined to produce petroleum, as I had imagined.

Having clarified this, Robert then related how he had been shown the set of Jenga I had given to his parents and, having played it, how he now loved the game. I was as pleased then as I always am when Jenga acquires a new fan, and I am sure I would have said as much. Robert asked if I was selling the game in Canada and whether I would be interested in allowing him to add the game to his portfolio of food-oil products and so become Jenga's distributor in Canada. I told Robert that although I had no sales representative in Canada, some Canadians may have purchased a few games because Jenga was selling primarily by mail order in North America, through the various ads I had placed in the *Smithsonian* and *The New Yorker* magazines.

I couldn't picture how Jenga and edible oil would mix, until Robert explained that many of his customers were natural food stores. He believed they would be interested in retailing a game made of natural wood, especially if he were to offer to hold in-store demonstrations of the game.

I was immediately comfortable with this idea of Robert becoming a distributor for Jenga in Canada. Although I didn't know Robert at all, I thought I knew, and I certainly liked, his Californian countercultural, feel-good, and supportive family. Coming from a close-knit family myself, the easygoing manner in which his three sisters engaged with each other and with their parents had struck me as open and honest and guided by a basic integrity that had felt familiar.

Robert's offer to become Jenga's distributor in Canada appeared to promise just what I needed at the time—someone actively seeking new outlets for Jenga. In many respects, it felt like a helping hand being proffered by a family member, albeit a rather distant one.

In England I was making all contacts and sales entirely on my own. I had found that I couldn't afford to employ, even on commission, sales representatives, distributors, or any other kind of middleman. As a consequence, although sales were growing steadily through retail outlets and by mail order, I was still not selling as many games as I had hoped to sell or indeed needed to sell in order to turn a profit and start repaying my loans.

In North America, I had succeeded in placing the game in a few stores, but Jenga was still selling primarily by mail order. My brother, Graham, and his wife, Sharon, continued to hold a stock of the games in their garage at home in Kentucky, and they kindly fulfilled orders and re-orders as they trickled in. But, as Graham worked incredibly long hours as a young physician and Sharon was fully occupied as a first-time mother, neither my brother nor his wife had spare time to actively seek new outlets for the game.

At first, Robert offered to purchase some of the stock I had stored in my brother's home, and I agreed to sell these to him at cost, with little or no markup, in order to allow him to test the game with the natural food stores where he had most of his contacts. Although such an arrangement was unusual, I thought it was a good business decision at the time. I was fully aware that I would be forgoing profits, but I was prepared to do this for a while in order to give Robert the opportunity to try to open up a market for Jenga in Canada. I also assumed that, if this trial run was a success, Robert and I would come to a different, more usual arrangement, one in which our share of the costs and profits would properly reflect our roles—mine as author and publisher of an established game and Robert as a distributor in Canada selling that game. But this is not quite what happened.

The Second Step

In the spring of 1985, a few months after Robert began distributing Jenga in Canada, he called me with a new proposal. He now wanted not only to expand the territory in which he could distribute Jenga to include North, South, and Central America, as well as Japan, but also to expand his role by acquiring the exclusive right to begin manufacturing and marketing Jenga in this territory.

Robert's spring proposal, which resulted in my signing the first of two agreements, coincided with a decision I had made a few months before, which was to give up on trying to cope on my own and to accept outside help. My resolve when I launched Jenga in 1983, to design, finance, develop, manufacture, market, and sell Jenga myself, had been sorely tested. I now had to face the fact that, though I had managed to do all I had planned and had successfully put the game on the market and Jenga was beginning to gain a momentum of its own, I was in such a financial pickle that I couldn't afford to reinvest in new stock. I realized that I would soon find myself in the absurd situation of being unable to afford producing even those games for which I had secured firm orders.

My once firm and resolute determination to go it alone had begun to wobble. Indeed, it had become so shaky that, when Camphill offered to manufacture Jenga at their own expense, in return for paying me an author's royalty of 6 percent on each game sold, I leapt at their generous offer. I stopped publishing Jenga myself, and Camphill became Jenga's publisher, selling it through their own trade catalogue of their own wooden toys.

Apart from the financial imperative, it's quite possible that I was finally ready to contemplate the idea of having someone else publish Jenga because, by this point, I had had the positive experience of working with an established publisher on another game. Toward the end of 1984, Sara Finch and I had created the Great Western Railway Game, which, from the outset, was to be published and distributed by Gibson Games Ltd.

Because of these satisfactory arrangements, using a publisher was no longer the anathema it had once been for me. Thus, Robert's suggestion that he manufacture, market, and distribute the game as its publisher in this expanded territory seemed like a reasonable idea. I remember thinking a short while later that I could relax, with Camphill looking after Europe and Robert tackling the Americas—and Japan.

As startling as this admission is for me to make now, as far as I can tell from any correspondence I have on file, it didn't appear to concern me that Robert seemed to have an utterly different approach to the business of publishing my games from that of Camphill or Gibson Games. Yet the contrast was stark, and it still puzzles me now that this did not set off any alarm bells. For starters, Robert mailed me a formal, twenty-page contract drawn up by a Californian intellectual property lawyer. My experiences with Camphill and Gibson Games could not have been more different.

Since the inception of Jenga, Camphill and I had had a relaxed working relationship that I had always appreciated was unusual, but it was a long time before I realized that it was in fact totally remarkable. Initially, Camphill had simply produced Jenga bricks for me to order, and I had paid them on receipt of each shipment of bricks. But even after Camphill became Jenga's publisher and paid me an author's royalty on each game sold, we had no written contract that I'm aware of. And Camphill claimed no rights to the game. Yet they were prepared to take the same financial risks and commit to the same marketing efforts as they would with a product that they could call entirely their own— Flappy Duck, for example.

The story of the Great Western Railway Game, which I discuss in detail later, is quite different from Jenga's story. From the outset, Sara and I were to author the game and Gibson Games would publish it under its own imprint Gibson Games was a long-established, family-owned firm, well regarded in the toy trade. Publishing a game under the Gibson Games' name guaranteed its success. Even so, as it was with Camphill, Gibson Games' agreement was essentially a tacit one. If there was a written contract with Gibson Games (and I can't find one on file), it's likely to have been a single-page document briefly stating the company's intention to publish and distribute the game and pay us a 5 percent royalty as authors of the game, for this is what the company did for many years. And all our development costs, as well as all their marketing, administrative, and managerial expenses, were on Gibson Games' tab.

The contrast between Robert's contract and requests and what Camphill and Gibson required should have sounded warning bells. If it did, their toll fell on deaf ears. I blithely signed this first agreement, and an even more substantial subsequent one, without seeking the advice of a lawyer in England or the United States.

Looking at both these documents today, I can only wonder at what possessed me in April 1985, and then five months later, in October of that same year, to sign away so much for so very little. By October 17, 1985, I had assigned *all* my rights in Jenga—including my trademark, copyright, and know-how rights—to Robert Grebler for his exclusive use worldwide and on the terms as presented.

The first agreement, dated April 16, 1985, makes no reference to Robert having paid me anything at all for giving him all these rights to Jenga for the Americas and Japan. Not a bean—not even an advance against royalties. What it does state is that, in essence, Robert was to manufacture and sell the game (i.e., publish it) in this territory and that he would pay me a 5 percent royalty on actual receipts from those sales. Furthermore, if he should sublicense anyone else to manufacture and sell the game, I would receive 20 percent of any actual royalties received by Robert, minus "reasonable" administration and management expenses incurred by him.

At the time of the first agreement in spring of 1985, I believed from my conversations and correspondence with Robert that he fully intended to publish Jenga himself. I must therefore have assumed that in due course I would be receiving an author's 5 percent royalty on all sales Robert made in the territory he had been assigned.

Such a royalty percentage would have been well in line with the amount Camphill would pay me as the author of Jenga and what Gibson Games would pay Sara and me as the authors of the Great Western Railway Game. I can only assume that it was this aspect of the agreement that diverted my attention from focusing on the underlying value of all the rights I had granted Robert. It may explain, too, why I never questioned Robert about why he needed any of these rights to publish Jenga, when Camphill had asked for none to publish the same game. Or indeed, why Robert would expect me to pay a percentage of his administration and management costs when neither Camphill nor Gibson Games expected any such contribution.

The Third Step

Whether Robert had intended to publish Jenga himself or not quickly became immaterial. Not long after I had signed that first agreement in April, Robert contacted me to tell me that he had convinced two of his older cousins, Paul Eveloff and David Grebler, to join him as partners to help him with Jenga and that together they had formed a partnership called Pokonobe Associates. Robert clearly respected these two men and considered bringing them into his business a major coup. Robert then told me that Pokonobe Associates was in contact with one of Canada's largest toy companies, with which Robert and his cousins believed they could secure an incredibly exciting publishing contract for Jenga. However, to enable Pokonobe Associates to secure this deal, I would now need to extend to worldwide all the rights I had assigned to Robert in April. Robert informed me if I were to assign these worldwide rights to him, he would then assign them to Pokonobe Associates, which, in turn, would assign publishing rights to the toy company.

I have no recollection of what Robert actually said in order to persuade me to assign him these worldwide rights. However, I must have assumed that either Pokonobe Associates had exclusive access to the toy company or that the toy company's offer to publish Jenga was in some way conditional on the toy company's being allowed to deal exclusively with Pokonobe Associates and not directly with me. Certainly, though I was informed some time later that year that the company interested in Jenga was Irwin Toy, I had no direct contact with anyone at Irwin Toy until some time after Irwin Toy had acquired the publishing rights to Jenga.

Over the years, I gradually came to form the impression that, from the start, Pokonobe Associates chose to play down my role as the author of Jenga. This impression, as I discovered recently, was not without justification. Hal Ross, whose story follows later, was an executive at Irwin Toy in 1985. It was Hal, as I have learned, who approached Robert about Jenga and not the other way around, as I had believed until fairly recently. In an interview early this year, Hal told me, "I thought Robert and the other two had said, 'We found this girl from Africa and she brought it to us to put it on the market.' That's what I remember they said to me."

Whatever may have happened at the time now needs to be put into perspective. I don't think I have an overinflated sense of my own self-worth, but I'm no wilting flower, either. I had had confidence enough—the outright chutzpah, even—to see Jenga and several other projects through every step of the way, from novel idea to actual sales. Hence my behavior at the time still puzzles me.

Why ever did I think that Robert, Paul, and David—three men I had never met—should step in and take over Jenga? I can only surmise that Robert must have been very persuasive.

Perhaps I was also ready to be persuaded. People often suppose that Jenga's success must be a great surprise to me, and they tell me "You couldn't have ever dreamed at the start that it would be *such* a hit." Well, all I can say is that they couldn't be more wrong. Like most designers, I had set out with a grand vision that my creation would be a worldwide sensation. And like all entrepreneurs, I had believed sincerely that I could make this vision a reality. I think this firm (if sometimes misguided) belief in yourself and your products is what defines the creative entrepreneur. So, although I was exceedingly grateful to the people of Camphill, there was a nagging concern that in accepting their offer to publish Jenga, I may have been limiting the game's potential to the capacity of a small-scale workshop and thus scaling down my aspirations for the game.

Robert's first offer to publish in the Americas and Japan would have brought Jenga to a much wider market, and Pokonobe Associates' offer to sublicense Jenga to Irwin Toy would have increased this market even further.

In essence, Robert managed to persuade me to assign him rights to my game because I believed that he shared the big dream I had for my game. And I assumed that if he believed in Jenga as I did, then he and his cousins would have the necessary commitment, drive, and skills to put my dream back on track—for me.

I was prepared to assume all this without doing any due diligence and without determining what Robert and his cousins' roles would be in the process. I did so, I think, because I was confident that my close friendship with Robert's sister was the only guarantee I needed that Pokonobe Associates would always champion me, as well as my game, and have my best interests at heart, as well as my game's.

As Robert is quoted as saying, "I think because of the family relationship we had, Leslie knew that she could trust me. We were lucky" (Walsh, *The Playmakers*, 247).

Lucky indeed!

The above may explain to some degree why I signed two agreements with Robert, but an important question remains: why did I come to believe that the terms of these two agreements would be considered unreasonable by anyone's measure?

My experience with Jenga is unique in many regards. But as any creative person taking an idea to market has to go through a process that is similar enough to mine, I think an analysis of what happened with Jenga may be useful to many other would-be entrepreneurs. I think this analysis may be done best by defining and expanding on the varying and typical roles of the author, editor, agent, and publisher in the process of bringing a game to market, and comparing that process with the analogous process of writing and publishing a book.

INTERESTINGLY (AND IMPORTANTLY), within both the book and game publishing worlds, the customary split in royalties between an author and his agent is a minimum of 80 percent for the author and a maximum of 20 percent for the agent. Now, in my case, Pokonobe Associates receives almost 80 percent and I receive a little over 20 percent of the royalties that the publisher (first Irwin Toy, now Hasbro) pays for Jenga. Whether this is to be considered a fair deal (in the common sense of the word) or not depends very much on the respective roles that Robert (and/or Pokonobe Associates) and I played in the early history of the game. Here, a brief excursion into books will be useful to examine the customary roles of author, editor, agent, and publisher.

Since the invention of the printing press in 1436, millions of books have been written and published. As a result, there are precedents, tried and tested, for author, editor, agent, and publisher to use as guidelines when negotiating the terms of any contract. The editor of a book may play a critical part in the development process of a book (I have learned just how critical writing this one). But there is never any suggestion that such editor should be considered its coauthor and therefore entitled to a percentage of the royalties due to the writer. And, however experienced and influential the author's agent might be, he is unlikely to expect more than 15 percent or, at the very most, 20 percent of what his client, the author, receives from the publisher in royalties from the sales of the finished work. In other words, it is normal practice for the publisher to pay the editor a fee dependent on the time taken to edit the book. And for the publisher to pay the author between 5 and 10 percent royalty on each book sold. And then for the author to pay her agent a royalty of 10 to 20 percent of what she receives. For example, say the publisher sells a book for $10; the author's 10 percent would be

$1 on each book sold. The author will subsequently pay her agent 20 cents for this book, if the author's agent's royalty is 20 percent.

Within the world of publishing games, the process of taking an idea to market follows along much the same lines as in books, with an author, editor, agent, and publisher playing very similar roles. However, within the games publishing world, there are more instances in which the lines between author (inventor), editor (developer), and agent have become blurred. In such cases, those who might otherwise be considered a game's editor or agent have become so involved in the design of the final product that sometimes, even justifiably, they expect recognition as its coauthor or more. Accordingly, that individual is no longer "just" the intermediary or facilitator between creator and publisher.

The game of Yahtzee is one such example. As its story goes, this now famous dice game was devised aboard a yacht by its owners, a wealthy Canadian couple who wished, for reasons never explained, to remain anonymous. Apparently, they contacted the toy industry veteran Edwin Lowe, who had already made a fortune selling Bingo, and asked him to manufacture for them, exclusively, one thousand copies of their "Yacht Game." In return for that service, they would grant him all rights to their game. Lowe obliged. A few years later, in 1956, Lowe devised, published, and launched a game based on the original game, which he renamed and trademarked Yahtzee. With his considerable experience of the toy business, Lowe was confident enough in the game's potential to risk almost a million dollars manufacturing, marketing, and advertising Yahtzee. It took a while, but the risk paid off. By the early 1970s, Yahtzee was so successful that Milton Bradley purchased Lowe's company (E. S. Lowe) simply to acquire the game.

Edwin Lowe may not have created the original game, but by virtue of his creative contribution to the final product, I believe he certainly warrants being credited as Yahtzee's coauthor. And, in having manufactured and marketed the game, he is undeniably its first publisher.

Scrabble's story is similar to Yahtzee's in many ways, although its inventor was not a nameless, wealthy yacht owner but one Alfred Butts. An architect, Mr. Butts, finding himself out of work during the Great Depression, devised, made by hand, and sold a game that at first he called Lexiko and later called Criss-Cross Words. He did this for some seven years, with modest success, but stopped making the game in 1940.

In 1947, James Brunot (a former welfare officer) contacted Alfred Butts with a proposal, which Butts accepted. Thus, in return for a small author's royalty, Butts assigned all his rights in the game to Brunot. Crucially, James Brunot redesigned the board, changed some rules, renamed it "Scrabble," and from 1949 to 1952, manufactured and sold the game through his own business, the Production & Marketing Corp.

In 1952, unable any longer to cope with the growing demand for the game, Brunot licensed Scrabble to Selchow & Righter. Over the years, Selchow & Righter sold millions and millions of sets of Scrabble (1 million in 1954 alone) until the company was purchased by Coleco in 1986, which in its turn was then bought by Hasbro three years later.

In the case of Scrabble, as it was for Yahtzee's Mr. Lowe, Mr. Brunot's creative input amply justifies an acknowledgment that, at the very least, he is a major author of Scrabble. Likewise, although it had been published previously by Mr. Butts as "Criss-Cross Words," Brunot was the first to manufacture and sell the game as Scrabble, so it would seem only fair to give him credit as Scrabble's first publisher, too.

I have told the stories of Yahtzee and Scrabble to provide a backdrop to the story of Jenga. In contrast, in the early history of Jenga, there is no one who plays a role equivalent to Yahtzee's Mr. Lowe or Scrabble's Mr. Brunot. In Jenga's story, there is a direct line from author to publisher that is anything but blurred.

I myself created the game, named the game, and published the game. Jenga was in production and on the market and selling in several countries around the world when Robert Grebler first approached me to distribute it for me. And it was this very game, as it stood, which

Pokonobe Associates sublicensed to Irwin Toy in order for them to publish it. In other words, Pokonobe Associates cannot claim credit as even minor coauthors or editors of Jenga. Nevetheless, it has in effect, and at times in substance, received credit as Jenga's primary author. Moreover, Pokonobe Associates has and does receive the rewards that go with such an accreditation.

Before discussing the specifics of my agreement with Robert, I should say that Robert's negotiations with me for the worldwide rights to Jenga were concurrent with both his negotiations with Pokonobe Associates *and* also with Pokonobe Associates' negotiations with Irwin Toy of Canada. I was not unaware of this chain at the time. I mention it to underscore the point that, *from the outset*, Pokonobe Associates intended to sublicense its rights in Jenga to Irwin Toy for Irwin Toy to publish the game. Interestingly, these were rights in a "property" that Pokonobe Associates did not even own during its negotiations with Irwin Toy, until, that is, a few days before Pokonobe Associates assigned them on to Irwin Toy.

In an agreement I signed on October 17, 1985, I assigned the worldwide rights in Jenga to Robert Grebler in return for 22.5 percent of any future royalties Pokonobe Associates was to receive from sublicensing the publishing rights in Jenga. Within sixty days of signing the agreement, I was to be paid a £2,000 (approximately $3,000) advance against these royalties.

I have on file an early draft master agreement between Pokonobe Associates and Irwin Toy in which Pokonobe Associates acknowledges that it has already received *"a non-recoverable advance in respect of the Royalty in the amount of $50,000 in United States funds"* and that Irwin Toy will pay Pokonobe Associates a *"second non-recoverable advance in respect of the Royalty in the amount of $65,000 in United States funds"* within thirty days after the date of execution of the agreement.

The contract goes on to say that in consideration of the ongoing exclusive rights and licenses that Pokonobe Associates had granted to them, Irwin Toy would pay Pokonobe Associates a royalty of 8 percent of net sales in Canada, 60 percent of all royalties it (Irwin Toy) received under any U.S. product sublicense, and 50 percent on royalties it (Irwin Toy) received under any sublicenses in countries other than Canada and the United States.

So, hypothetically, if Irwin Toy were to sell a game it published in Canada for $10, Pokonobe Associates would receive 80 cents from Irwin Toy. Pokonobe Associates would then give me 18 cents and keep 62 cents for itself. (In reality, I would receive still less than this because Pokonobe usually retains a further percentage to cover its "administration and management costs.")

I came to regret signing away my rights to Jenga on those terms when it finally dawned on me that Pokonobe Associates was receiving what would traditionally be an author's share but had done little, if anything, more than act as an agent between me, Jenga's author, and Irwin Toy, Jenga's publisher. It was as though Robert, Paul, and David had *each* individually contributed as much or even slightly more than I had to the creation of Jenga. But this was very far from the truth. When I signed that first agreement in April 1985, Robert could justly take credit for selling sets of Jenga in Canada. However, it cannot be said in all fairness that at that time Robert had had any hand in *creating* the game that I assigned him rights to publish in the Americas and Japan. And neither, in all fairness, can it be said that Pokonobe Associates added anything of tangible value to the game it acquired from me in October 1985 and concurrently sublicensed to Irwin Toy—certainly not anything that could be construed as having authored the game.

Robert, Paul, and David had changed no rules of play for Jenga; nor had they renamed the game; nor had they manufactured the game; nor had they repackaged the game when Irwin Toy first saw and expressed interest in Jenga. Pokonobe Associates may have spent some money on setting up its own business and on visiting Irwin Toy and on lawyers' fees in drawing up contracts, but the three partners had invested little or nothing in the game itself before assigning the sublicense to Irwin Toy. Yet, Pokonobe Associates managed to negotiate with Irwin Toy the significant nonrefundable advance of $115,000, and a very generous author's royalty percentage of 8 percent—77.5 percent of which it could keep—all for doing little more than brokering a deal. It was, in fact, the kind of deal that would be expected of any good agent, but on behalf of and to the benefit of his client, the author.

Although I came to believe many years ago that the agreement between Pokonobe Associates and me is way off balance, I would probably have remained silent on this issue if it were not for something that was said to me while I was researching this book. I went to New York to interview Alan Hassenfeld, the chairman of Hasbro Corporation, which has produced Jenga under license since early 1986. Alan introduced me to Phil Jackson, the executive head of the games division. It is under Phil's auspices that Hasbro sells almost 2 million sets of Jenga each year. Phil confessed, over a cup of coffee, that although he knew Pokonobe Associates well, he had previously never heard of me and had no idea that anyone other than the "Pokonobe boys" had been involved in the development of Jenga.

This comment shocked me even more than Hal Ross telling me that he had believed in 1985 that I had taken the game to Pokonobe Associates "to put on the market." It shocked me enough to force me finally to think about how and why Pokonobe Associates has never—until very recently—made a point of stressing my authorship of the game, and has never integrated into their marketing and selling strategy the fact that the game has a living author. One would think to do so would have been very much in the interests of Jenga. In my opinion, there is just one conclusion to draw, which is that Pokonobe Associates must feel that it was not in its own interest to attract attention to the fact that I am the sole author of the original game of Jenga.

Hard, but Useful, Lessons Learned

I hope that clarifying the provenance of Jenga will not put at risk my greatly valued friendship with Gill. It is ironic that my relationship with her, which allowed me to place my trust in Robert in the first instance, also kept me silent long after I had begun to feel that such trust was misplaced. But the process of writing this book has made it increasingly clear to me that ignoring or glossing over the contents and terms of the assignment of Jenga and its implications is not an option. If I were to talk about the remarkable business of creating Jenga in any meaningful way, I had to remark on *all* the problems I faced and comment on all the insights I gained. Exploring this particular part of Jenga's story has been quite a painful process, and I am not sure even now that I have identified all the reasons for doing what I did. I have recognized, however, that there were lessons learned, albeit the hard way, that I have put into practice since and can now pass on.

Obviously, if anyone presents you with a contract—however close your relationship—consult your own lawyer before you sign.

Another, more subtle, lesson is the need to realize that business functions smoothly only if we can rely on trust and fair play among the parties collaborating. Still, we need to recognize that because each of us has a responsibility to look after his or her own interests and stand up for his or her own rights, in business, not all players play by the same set of rules.

EAST AFRICA (1932–1973)

My mother crouching down on the steps of Chiwanjee with her brother Bill, and two little friends. Their ayahs (nannies) are in watchful attendance behind. 1932

My mother waiting to one side while her father repairs the vehicle. Safaris in Tanganyika in the '30s were punctuated at regular intervals with mending punctures or broken axles or pushing the truck out of the mud. 1939

My father, age 18, then a spitfire pilot and officer of The Royal Air Force. 1940

My mother, age 20, typing outside her banda (hut) in Mgulani Camp, the temporary accommodation for Tanganyika government employees in Dar-es-Salaam. 1949

Me, age six months, with my ayah, Paula, in Kurasini, Dar-es-Salaam, before I had any hair. 1956

Me, Father, Sue, Graham, holding Malcolm, and Mother. Nairobi, Kenya. 1971

My brothers, Graham (with shark) and Malcolm, in Vipingo, Kenya. 1972

Me playing football. Evidence that I did indulge in some sporting activity from time to time. Taunton School, Somerset. 1973

WEST AFRICA (1973–1975)

My father and Otumfuo Nana, Opoku Ware II, the Asantehene (King of the Ashanti). Kumasi, Ghana. 1974

My sister, Sue, in Ougadouga, The Republic of Upper Volta (now Burkina Faso) on safari from Accra, Ghana. 1975

Photograph of a boxed set of an early version of Jenga made to order for us in Takoradi, Ghana. 1973 (photograph by Sue Macpherson ARPS)

ENGLAND (1975–1998)

Jerome Fletcher walking the Somerset plains under flood. 1975

Oxford University's Real Tennis Court in which we held the "Elizabethan feast" when Jerome was the professional. 1982

The very first sets of Jenga were stacked and packed into made-to measure clear plastic cartons. To avoid the expense of printing on the carton, this sheet was slipped inside, and was visible along one side. 1982

Publicity shot of me playing Jenga. 1982
(photograph by Sue Macpherson ARPS)

The Oxford Times *Jenga Tournament at the Randolph Hotel, Oxford.*
1983 (photograph by Sue Macpherson ARPS)

Sara Finch, Arabella Kiszley, and me with the Great Western Railway Game, Swipe, Jenga, and
Good Gift *magazine. This was from a photo shoot for an article in the* Guardian
newspaper. 1985 (photograph by Sue Macpherson ARPS)

Playing Takoradi Bricks

Sir — *The Oxford Times* 'Jenga' Tournament was shrouded, at least for this reader, in a suitable cloak of mystery until the photographs of combat appeared in last week's paper.

I know this very game as "Takoradi Bricks", named after the major seaport of Ghana. During the Second World War, Spitfire aircraft were shipped there in kit form for assembly before being flown (effectively a test flight) to Egypt for the North African campaign. The RAF engineers and pilots in Takoradi adopted (or as I thought — perhaps mistakenly — invented) the game of building and withdrawing wooden bricks to while away the long hours of boredom between shipments and flights.

I myself was first introduced to the game in October 1979 during a stay in Ghana, when I was invited for a social evening at the British High Commission in Accra, the capital.

Incidentally, the game seems to be known only to the British in Ghana; my attempts to buy a set of Takoradi Bricks in the streets of Accra were met with bewilderment — this, despite a vigorous and enterprising grapevine amongst the marketeers which sought to supply equally obscure merchandise not in stock. (I remember one day buying a second-hand copy of *Journey Without Maps*, Graham Greene's marvellous tale of travel through Liberia. To while away my own leisure time, I and a friend asked, without success, in various parts of the same market for other Greene novels. A week or so later, however, when I was visiting a market in quite another part of the city, a complete stranger summoned me with the typical hissing *Sssssst* and whispered "You want to buy some Graham Greene?"

All of which leaves me pondering the origin of "Jenga," and to suggest that if nobody knows, a word in the ear of the Accra market would surely yield a swift answer.

EUAN DUNN

Bornholm Farm,
Chawley Lane,
Cumnor

OXFORD TIMES '83

Those Takoradi Bricks

Sir — I was very interested to read the 'Takoradi Bricks' letter from Mr Dunn in *The Oxford Times* last week. This is one of several letters I have received (in the past few months from people who have come across a version of the game before. Explanations of the origin of the game are proliferating — one minute it was born in East Africa, the next in Holland and the next in West Africa. One person claims it is being made by Kenyan Handicapped People, another that the British Leyland plant in Ghana are manufacturing sets!

The following is an explanation of the origin of the game Jenga, to the best of my knowledge:

My parents moved to Accra in 1972 from Nairobi. Sometime after their arrival they bought a set of building blocks, handmade by a Ghanaian in Takoradi. As Mr Dunn points out, the game was not played by native Ghanaians, so I think I would be right in assuming that the bricks were not sold as a game. A version of the game, which we did call Takoradi Bricks, developed from the game which many children play with dominoes. It was then played with friends in the expatriate community of Accra. This is one I brought a set back to Oxford in 1973 where, along with the friends I lived with, formal rules were developed and we started calling the game *Jenga*.

Jenga is played in a subtly but significantly different way from the original version and an essential part of the game is that each brick must be different either in size or weight.

An interesting aspect of the story Mr Dunn relates is the RAF connection. Another correspondent mentions that he thought the game had been invented by two RAF pilots in Kenya. My father was a Spitfire pilot in the RAF during the war, though he worked for an oil company in Accra. I wonder if this could be a case of an International Game of Chinese Whispers!

LESLIE SCOTT

7 Bath Street,
St Clement's,
Oxford.

20 MAY 1983

Reproduced by kind permission of The Oxford Times

All three editions of the Good Gift *magazine published by LSA Publications.
1984 and 1985* (photograph by Sue Macpherson ARPS)

*My husband, Professor Fritz
Vollrath, a zoologist and great
advocate of curiosity-driven
research. 1989* (photograph
by Sue Macpherson ARPS)

A selection of games from OGL's The Oxford Games Collection. 1998 (photograph by Sue Macpherson ARPS)

Our children, Frederica and Digby. 1993

EAST AFRICA (present day)

The house that Jenga built. Jenga House, Mpala Research Centre, Laikipia, Kenya. 2001 (photograph by Sue Macpherson ARPS)

NINE

The Learning Curve

Once a game of Jenga has come tumbling down, it is no longer possible to tell from looking at the scattered bricks which brick had been supporting which other brick before the tower fell. Looking back on the years immediately following my launch of the game, it would appear, even to me, that I was engaged in all sorts of odd and seemingly unrelated activities during that period. Yet, like the individual bricks of the game, each activity must have underpinned another and played a supporting role in the overall construction of Jenga.

If Jenga had not become the success it is today, I would suggest that it might be wise to read my story of its early history as a guide to how *not* to put a game on the market. But as Jenga did work, maybe it would be more helpful if I were to tease out the elements I think may have contributed to its success. It could be argued that what I'm aiming to do in this book is first reconstruct a sequence of events and then deconstruct it to make some sense of it all.

Keeping Above Water

When I was a child, my family frequently went on trout-fishing expeditions on one of the rivers that run off Mount Kenya in the north or off Mount Elgon in the west of Kenya. I loved these safaris to these wild spots, not because I was any good at fly-fishing—trout had little to fear from me—but I liked nothing better than playing a game my siblings and I had devised that involved racing each other up the middle of the river by jumping from one rocky outcrop to another. Though fast flowing, these clear mountain streams were never very deep, so I guess there was no great danger in this particular sport. I found it thrilling nonetheless, deciding which course to take, which obstacles to avoid or which to jump over, and making snap judgments about the suitability of the next rock. Would it be too wet and slippery or too far to reach safely, or would it perhaps leave me stranded, having to retrace my jumps? It was exciting, exhausting, and fun.

Looking back, I can make more sense of what I did in the first few years following the launch of Jenga in 1983 if I visualize it as a version of the Trout River Game, jumping from one rock to another in a frantic attempt to avoid slipping into a river of debt. Although on occasion I misjudged a jump, it was exciting, exhausting, and fun—most of the time.

Despite having on file all my old diaries and much of my correspondence (albeit with mouse- or, even worse, rat-chewed corners) as an aide-mémoire, I have found it difficult to sort out the chronological order of the various enterprises I undertook in the wake of launching Jenga—perhaps for the simple reason that there was little order in the first place. I was hopping from one thing to the next.

Sales of the game were considerably less than I had first forecast. Actually, that's quite an understatement; I had anticipated selling five thousand in the first twelve months. I think I sold fewer than one thousand. Hence, toward the end of 1983 I was very short of cash, despite having sold my house and the Intel shares I had been given when I worked for the company. The proceeds from both had been invested (sunk) into the business of producing, marketing, and selling Jenga. I had to return to the bank to seek an addition to the government-backed loan granted to me to get the business up and running in the first instance.

In order to encourage banks to lend money to new businesses, the UK government had set up the "Small Firms Loan Guarantee Scheme," in which they would guarantee 80 percent of a bank's loan to a fledgling business. As luck would have it, the scheme had only recently come into existence when I was seeking funding, and banks were enthusiastic about making these loans when I approached Lloyds the first time. It is highly unlikely that they would have lent me the £20,000 I sought in November 1982 either before or much after that date. Few of the businesses established in the early days of this scheme survived beyond a year, probably because many banks initially failed to apply sufficiently rigorous selection criteria, as they should have and later did, when they had much more to lose.

When I went back to the bank twelve months later, asking for more, they were totally unwilling to lend me any more unsecured funds. I was told that money would be available only if I could find someone to guarantee the additional loan.

Jerome offered to act as a guarantor for part of this increased loan. By having him deposit funds at my bank, the bank agreed to give me a back-to-back loan. That is, they were willing to lend me money up to the amount Jerome had put on deposit with them on the understanding that if I failed to repay my loan, they would clear the slate by helping themselves to his money. It was remarkable that Jerome agreed to do this. For, although we remained close, after seven years of living together, we had parted and gone our separate ways. Plus, he could ill afford it (his job as a Real Tennis professional, though unusual, was not extraordinarily well paid). And this was in addition to money that Jerome had already lent me.

My mother, too, backed yet another loan. In her case, she guaranteed it by allowing the bank to use her house as security.

The only defense I can offer for allowing my mother and my dearest friend to take such risks on my behalf is that I was absolutely certain that Jenga would be very successful in the end. And it was, but not before the bank called in all my loans and Jerome and my mother and the UK government had to honor their guarantees. In the long run I did manage to repay both my mother and Jerome (and via my taxes, the government too) with interest, but it must have been a very tense few years for them and there must have been the odd moment when they questioned their faith in me.

We remain to this day on very good terms—understandably, I guess, in my mother's case, blood being thicker than water and all that—but it continues to astonish me that Jerome didn't sever connections long ago. One of the documents to have survived the mice and the rats and the foxing because of the dampness is a copy of a letter from Lloyds Bank North Cheam to Jerome F., Esq.:

Dear Sir,

I have to inform you that our customer Leslie Ann Scott, has, after a request for payment, failed to repay the amount owing to the Bank and I am, therefore, instructed to call upon you for payment under your guarantee dated 15th June 1984 of £5,000 being the amount of your liability thereunder.

Under the terms of your Guarantee, interest runs at 2 percent above the Bank's Base Rate with quarterly rests on the sum of £5,000 from the date of this Demand until payment. However, as cash was deposited in support of your Guarantee, I have applied this in settlement of your liability.

Yours faithfully,
C.P Barrett
Manager
c.c. R.H.O
Realizations Dept.

The Realizations Department? The mind boggles. Is this the room in a bank where the penny finally drops? Five thousand pounds was a serious amount of money at the time. To put it in context, I bought my house in 1982 for £12,000. The same house, I noticed in the property section of the local paper, was valued at £300,000 in 2008. Admittedly, this was before the credit crunch crashed house prices, but it would still fetch something in that order today.

I'm ashamed to admit that I must have blanked that letter from my mind, as I have no recollection of what I felt or what Jerome said when he received and read its chilling content. But I don't need any moldy piece of paper to remind me of two other encounters I had as a result of being up to my ears in debt.

A little while after Jerome and I had separated and I had sold my house, I rented a cheerful little cottage promisingly called Golden Square, situated down a very narrow lane in a remote village on the edge of the Cotswolds. Grossly underestimating the work involved, I had agreed to look after the cottage's three-acre garden in lieu of much of the rent. What I had thought of as a terrific bargain and a clever move turned out to be a very expensive mistake, because I ended up having to employ a full-time gardener just to keep the grass cut and the weeds at bay. However, one advantage of the place was that it had a small stone shed attached to the house in which I was able to set up my office. For a brief time, Golden Square was the Jenga headquarters.

Working at my desk one morning I was surprised to see a middle-aged man, dressed in a suit, walk in through the gate and up to my front door. Few people called to see me without notice, even fewer on foot. I went out to greet him.

"Miss Scott?" he inquired as I approached.

"Yes. Good morning. How may I help?"

"Miss Leslie Ann Scott?" he said, looking down at the clipboard that he held in his hand.

"Yes?"

"Miss Scott, are you the owner of a blue Alpha Romeo with the registration number DBH 532T?" he asked, looking toward the sporty car with this registration number, incongruously parked in my driveway. This was the very car that I had bought with a loan from a credit agency when I was still working for Arena and had a regular salary and could afford the monthly repayments.

"Yes. Why do you ask?"

"Well, Miss Scott, I represent Lombards. I'm afraid to say that I believe there is a small matter of . . . er . . . um, er . . . some payments outstanding and I have been sent to retrieve this vehicle."

"Oh dear," I said. "How very embarrassing. I knew I was a little behind. I didn't realize it was that bad. Look, I was just about to make myself a cup of tea. Would you care to join me?"

"That's very kind. Thank you. I don't mind if I do."

Sitting at the kitchen table sipping on tea and munching on the couple of biscuits I had managed to rustle up, I said, looking across at this very pleasant, slightly built, and well-dressed man, "Please. Don't think me rude, but in your . . . um . . . line of work, wouldn't being a little larger, a little more bulky, and a lot more aggressive help. I can imagine that there are people who might get a little upset about having to hand the keys to their cars over to you."

"Oh, yes indeed, you're quite right. Some do get a little agitated when I call. It's not often I'm invited in and offered a cup of tea before I take a vehicle away."

"Well, what do you do if, say, they get a little physical? If you don't mind my asking?" I was genuinely intrigued.

"If you'll excuse me a moment, I'll show you," he said, getting up from the table and opening the front door.

"Brendan!" he called loudly from the doorway "Oh Bren—dan!" And from around the hedge and in through the gate strode an incredibly solid and rather menacing-looking young man.

Turning to me, my Alpha's repossessor said with a sweet smile, "If it looks like there might be a spot of bother, I call Brendan to give me a hand."

Possibly a little disappointed that his services as backup strong man were not required that day, Brendan glowered at me while, without protest, I meekly gave the Alpha's keys to his bantamweight colleague and then watched as they both drove away in the car. I never heard another thing about DBH 532T. I assume it was sold for as much, if not more, than the £2,796 loan still outstanding when they came to take it away.

The other encounter with a debt collector I will never forget—nor, I imagine, will my dear mother—took place eight or nine months later, when I had given up the cottage, which I could no longer afford, and my mother, out of the goodness of her heart, had "temporarily" taken me in.

When my father died soon after retiring to England, my mother had bought and moved into a very beautiful Cotswold Stone house just outside of Oxford called Rimes House. Ironically, given the story I'm about to tell, *rime* in Old English can mean "to count," and it is believed the house was called Rimes House (the counting house) because it had in the early seventeenth century been home to the bailiff of a country estate. For six months or so, I lived in my mother's house, along with my grandmother and younger brother, and had an office in the attic.

Up there one morning, I heard my mother call up the stairs, "Leslie. There's a gentleman to see you."

Something in the way she had said "gentleman" conveyed a note of anxiety, so I hurried down the stairs.

Standing in the flagstone hallway was a very official-looking man in a tailored gray overcoat carrying a black briefcase. *Oops*, I thought. *Now what have I done?*

"Miss Leslie Ann Scott?" the man said.

"Yes?" I replied.

"Miss Scott. I am a bailiff," he said, showing me an identify card.

"Oh. I see. Would you like to come through and sit down?" I asked, leading him into the sitting room, where I offered him a seat.

"Now, what can I do for you?"

"It would appear that you are in considerable arrears with your Visa card payments, and I have been sent to collect what you owe."

"I think there has been some mistake," I said. "Granted, I *was* in arrears, but I believe I am totally up to date now." I had borrowed yet more money from my mother to pay this debt, so I knew that what I was saying was true.

I left the bailiff drinking a cup of tea with my ninety-five-year-old grandmother, who remarkably sharp and always keen to be kept in the loop, had joined us in the sitting room, and I dashed upstairs to get the paperwork to prove my innocence.

When he saw it, he asked if he might use a phone. He made a quick call and confirmed that all was as I had said; the debt had been cleared. His information was out of date and he had been sent to see me in error.

"I'm very sorry, this has never happened before," he said. "Usually, I have the rather unpleasant duty of having to extract what is owed before I return."

"Goodness," I said. "And how do you do that if the person doesn't have the money?"

"As I am a bailiff appointed by the courts, I am entitled to remove belongings up to the value of what is owed."

"You can take anything you choose?"

"Anything, that is, except the tools of your trade and the bed you sleep in."

"And what if the bed I sleep in *is* one of the tools of my trade? Do I get to select something else you might take?" I asked a little cheekily, possibly light-headed with relief that he wasn't about to walk out with some of my mother's possessions.

He looked a little puzzled, though my grandmother laughed with delight.

Displacement Activity

I did make some attempt at supplementing my meager income from Jenga by taking on a couple of odd jobs, *odd* possibly being the operative word. Working for the sculptress Angela Conner was one, and becoming the Oxford representative for the National Theatre was another. Neither brought in very much money, but then neither engaged me for more than a few hours per week, and both gave me the opportunity to "broaden my contacts" for Jenga, or so I claimed in a letter to the bank. I do not have the manager's reply on file, but I can't imagine he was overly impressed by these particular line items as income in my cash flow forecast. Nevertheless, I believed that, as I couldn't afford to advertise the game in a more conventional manner, it was a good idea to be paid to do anything, however odd, which might contribute in any small way to promoting Jenga. Besides, I thoroughly enjoyed my time with both Angela and her husband, the documentary filmmaker John Bulmer. And I loved having an excuse to go regularly to the National Theatre in London. And I certainly did "broaden my contacts."

As the National Theatre rep, I was invited to see every play the theatre put on—gratis—and for the first year, if my 1984 diary is to be believed, I spent at least a night a week, often more, at one or another of the National's three theaters. Of the many, many plays I saw staged in the three years I worked for them, the most memorable were those starring either Ian McKellen or Anthony Hopkins, and Ingmar Bergman's production of *Hamlet* performed entirely in Swedish. The production was so enthralling that it didn't seem to matter that the only words I could understand were *prins* and *omlette.*

As Angela's assistant I found myself at all sorts of "horizon-broadening" events, though possibly none more unusual than a dinner held at the Polish Club hosted by Andrew, Duke of Devonshire, one of Angela's greatest patrons. In March 1982 a work of art commissioned by both houses of Parliament and sculpted by Angela had been erected on Thurloe Square opposite the Victoria and Albert Museum as a memorial to what the historian Nikolai Tolstoy refers to as "The victims of the Yalta Agreement." These were Russian exiles forcibly repatriated to Russia—where they would meet certain death—as a result of an agreement signed by Churchill, Roosevelt, and Stalin in Yalta in 1945 at the end of the war.

A few months after its installation, Angela's work, a tipping water sculpture, had been totally destroyed by vandals. Outraged, Count Tolstoy and many others, including Margaret Thatcher, had raised funds to replace the sculpture. The dinner at the Polish Club was held following a reception at the Victoria and Albert Museum where Angela was exhibiting a series of lithographs she had produced to be sold as part of this fund-raising drive. There I found myself seated next to a slight, dark man a couple of years older than myself who looked vaguely familiar and who pinched my bottom as I took my seat. This act so startled me I rounded on him and barked, "What the . . . ?"

Giving me a disconcertingly innocent sweet smile, the man drawled, "I'm so sorry. Did it hurt?"

"Yes! Well, no, not really. You insulted me."

"I'm Zera Yacob, you see. And you are?"

"Leslie Scott."

"Pleased to meet you. Do you come here often?"

"Do you mean the Polish Club? No, I have never been here before, and you?"

"'I?" he asked with an almost Gallic shrug, "I come here often."

"You're Polish?"

"Good heavens, no. Of course not. I am Ethiopian, but I had many Polish friends at Cambridge."

"Ethiopian? You must be Prince Zera Selassie? I saw the name on the guest list. Come to think of it, I hope you don't mind me saying, but you do look remarkably like your grandfather. You know, I once rode your grandfather's horses?"

"No, that I didn't know," he said with eyebrows raised. "Why? Where?"

"In Addis Ababa in 1965, when I was about ten years old. We spent three or four months living in the city very close to the emperor's palace, in fact in a hotel overlooking the royal stables. My sister and I went down to the stables every evening and admired the horses and the fantastic collection of gold and silver saddles and bridles in the air-conditioned tack room. We marveled at how in Ethiopia, horses were cared for far better than people."

"Did you, now?" the prince looked annoyed.

"Yes. There were staggering numbers of people living in awful conditions, and a notable number of horses living in luxury."

"Really?" The prince now looked bored.

"The head groom there grew quite fond of us and once even popped me up on a horse. I have a picture of myself astride an exquisite black stallion, and I frequently brag that I once rode Emperor Haile Selassie's horses."

"Do you? How very entertaining," the prince said sourly. "I rode them too as a child, but no longer. I've lived in exile now since 1974. Yes, despite the fact that I am Prince Zera Yacob Amha Selassie of the Royal House of Solomon and the Emperor Haile Selassie's grandson, I cannot go back to Ethiopia."

"Well, probably because you are."

"Because I am what?"

"You can't go back to Ethiopia because you are Prince Zera et cetera, et cetera, and the overthrown Emperor Haile Selassie's grandson."

"That's what I said."

"Actually, what you said was *despite* . . . But oh, never mind. Would you care for a pickled gherkin and a little more vodka?"

As I said, the income from these extracurricular activities was so paltry that it seems, on reflection, that I was probably engaged in some sort of "displacement activity," a term animal behaviorists use to describe the seemingly inappropriate actions an animal might perform while in a state of stress, frustration, or uncertainty. Birds, for example, often preen themselves when uncertain whether to attack or flee from an opponent; similarly, humans might scratch their heads when in doubt about what action to take. In my case, I took off to the theater or went to help sort out Angela's studio rather than confront the fact that I was at a loss about what to do next to promote Jenga after its less than successful and more than costly launch had soaked up most of my funds.

The Loose Leaf Collection

In my general ignorance of the toy business, I had believed that all I had to do with Jenga was to package it well and to introduce people to this marvelous game and the orders would come flooding in. Foolishly, it turned out, I had pinned all my hopes on Jenga's big debut at the London Toy Fair and had invested most of my initial funds into ensuring that everything was just right for that event. I was convinced that once buyers saw it, they would tumble over each other in their eagerness to put Jenga on the shelves in their shops. This is not quite what happened.

There is a section dedicated to toy trade newcomers within the exhibition hall of the London Toy Fair where the organizers make available standard, preconstructed booths at a bargain price. I had discovered that this area is ominously dubbed "death row" in the trade, as it is assumed that few of the products displayed ever see the light of day after the show ends. Very keen to avoid this fate for my new product, I had preferred to purchase space elsewhere in the hall and had elected for the expensive option of a custom-made stand that I had, of course, asked Arena to design and build. Somehow I had managed to dragoon my mother, my sister Sue, and several friends into "volunteering" to help me on the stand for the four days of the show. And I had then bullied them all into wearing something stylish and all black to match what I considered my stylishly all-black exhibition stand. And, anxious lest they not look keen and alert at all times, I had refused to allow any of my crew to sit. In fact, I had banished all chairs from sight. I placed an ad in the show's catalogue. I designed, printed, and distributed leaflets. I issued a press release. Then I and my team stood to attention, ready to deal with the people I was certain would flood on to our stand wishing to see the game I had publicized as "about to take the world by storm."

We may not have been condemned to sit on death row, but four days can seem an awfully long stretch if you are sentenced to spending it standing in a ten-foot by ten-foot by ten-foot black box trying to look cheerful and enthusiastic as you play endless games of Jenga on a *glass* tabletop, wilting in an all-black outfit under the heat of a dozen thousand-watt lights. Especially if few people show any interest and no one, *not one single person*, places an order for so much as a single game during the span of the show.

Unsettling though this was, I came home from the show having learned a number of invaluable lessons about trying to break into the toy trade. In the first instance, except for a couple of notable

exceptions, I discovered few game and toy buyers were actually interested in the intrinsic merits of a game per se. How much was being
committed to advertising was a great deal more important than how
the game or toy was played, and novelty was deemed a real drawback,
not at all the positive draw and selling point I had assumed.

Mr. Cooke, the founder and owner of the toy store Tridias, and Mr.
Dadabhoy, the adult games buyer of Harrods, were two notable exceptions who were interested in the game for the game's sake. Both men
had spotted Jenga at the toy fair and, although neither placed an order
on the day, both took the trouble to play the game and both decided to
stock it later that year. In fact, Tridias not only took it for their flagship
store in Bath but also placed it in their increasingly popular mail-order
catalogue, where they gave it prominent space and a sizable plug. As a
result, it sold well and became one of their staples. Harrods took the
game on the understanding that I would demonstrate it in the adult
games department in the run-up to Christmas.

Perhaps a little too late in the day, it finally dawned on me that the
majority of retail buyers simply would not, even *could not*, trade with
a fledgling, single-product company, however potentially exciting the
product. It was not economical for them to go about the business of
setting up an account, negotiating terms, and making delivery arrangements, let alone creating space within a store to stock a small quantity
of just the one untried, unknown product of an untried, unknown sup-
plier. I was advised that the only chance I had of getting Jenga into the
major retail stores was to place the game with a wholesaler who was
already selling to those stores—that, and run a serious promotional
campaign, neither of which I could afford to do.

On average, retail stores want to put a markup of 100 percent
on the price they pay for a product. In selling games directly to the
retailer, I was already selling at a unit price below what I really needed
to charge to cover my costs and make a profit. That profit, by the way,
was needed to be plowed straight back into the business. My price

should have been approximately double what I was paying Camphill to manufacture the game, which was £3. This meant that I should have been charging £6 and the retailer should have been charging £12 for the game. In fact, I was charging £5 and the retailer was charging £10.

For a middleman or wholesaler to earn the margins he would need to handle the game, either the final price tag on a game of Jenga in a shop would have been unacceptably high or my margin unworkably low.

I realized that the only way to significantly reduce the cost per unit was to increase production, that is, to commission Camphill to manufacture more games at any one time. But to commit to a higher production run with so few firm orders on my books was out of the question. Thus, I couldn't sell enough games because of its high unit price, yet I couldn't reduce the unit price because I couldn't sell enough games. It was a vicious circle and my first encounter with the phenomenon known as "the economies of scale." While a working appreciation of this concept certainly held me in good stead later in my career when costing and publishing Oxford Games' games, it would have been useful to have acquired this knowledge before I jumped into producing Jenga.

Whereas I certainly, if a little belatedly, had begun to appreciate some of the issues involved in producing and selling Jenga, I'm afraid I had yet to grasp the scale of the problems I faced in launching a product that was not just a new game but also possibly a whole new game concept. There was nothing on the market at the time to which it could be compared. The game of pick-up sticks (Mikado in Europe) was about the closest one might get, and that was not close at all.

Always very conservative, that year the toy market was particularly skittish about backing untried concepts. The lucrative and rapidly expanding video game market had suddenly begun to spiral into decline, taking manufactures and retailers with it. Atari, overeager for an even bigger share of the market, had seized an opportunity to cash in on the phenomenal success of Stephen Spielberg's 1982 film *E.T. The Extra-Terrestrial* and had launched an E.T. video game in time for Christmas. This was such a rushed job and so poorly conceived that it still ranks as one of the worst video games of all times. It bombed so badly that the company had to dispose of 5 million unsold or returned video cartridges, which according to legend, were taken out under cover of darkness and buried in a landfill site in Alamogordo, New Mexico. In order to keep the site from being looted, steamrollers crushed and flattened the games and a concrete slab was poured over the lot. The ignominious fate of these games left the games industry a touch shaken. No retailer was eager to attempt to guess what might be the next big thing and risk getting caught riding along on a runaway bandwagon.

As a way around this dilemma, I decided to try selling some games by mail order direct to the public. I justified this by arguing that ruling out both retailer and wholesaler meant that any one game sold by mail order was worth, to me, two or even three games sold through a good retail store. Cutting out the retailer allowed me to retain the retailer's markup. Plus, I would receive payment in advance, rather than after the typical delay of a month (or two or three) that I had come to expect and was forced to accept from the stores. In addition, I would be promoting the game, thereby going some way toward addressing the retailers' concern about the lack of publicity.

Although the concept of mail-order shopping for basic necessities had been around for many years in the United States, in the 1980s in the UK it had suddenly become positively chic to purchase upmarket goods by post. The high-end magazines, *Harpers and Queen*, *The Tatler*, and *Vogue*, all featured a "catalogue of catalogues" section in their October, November, and December issues in the run-up to Christmas. I decided to publish my own mail-order catalogue of gifts and promote it in these three glossy publications. I thought if I nestled my catalogue among a collection of those of some very fashionable and established organizations, I would catch the eye of the same discerning shopper who ordered her Christmas gifts from them.

Thus The Loose Leaf Collection was born. This comprised a set of colored postcards, each of which bore an artful photograph (by the then up-and-coming and now very-well-established photographer Andreas von Einsiedel) of an unusual gift for sale. Jenga, of course, was one. The others included the word game Swipe (more about this game later); an intriguing pair of brass candlesticks designed by Angela Conner; a limited edition print of a drawing of a horse, also by Angela; several items of silver jewelry designed and made by Tom Saddington; a rather ingenious handmade wooden letter rack and salad bowls by Tim Cole; and a pot of smoked eel paté by Brown and Forest. It was an idiosyncratic and rather odd collection, one might say "loose" in many respects. The only thing that bound them was that each of the producers, including the photographer, was a personal friend of mine.

I hesitate to claim that the concept—a catalogue consisting of a collection of arty postcards—was unique, as it is quite possible someone somewhere was doing something similar. However, I had never seen anything like this at the time. Art galleries and museums sold postcard reproductions of works of art, but using the postcard format to advertise a product was highly unusual. Four-color, glossy printing was exorbitantly expensive, and few printers had either the equipment or the expertise to produce art-quality postcards. Today, with digital photography and printing, it is a very different story, which explains why postcards now are used universally as a cheap and effective form of advertising, even given away free in cafés and clubs.

Even though The Loose Leaf Collection was not a roaring financial success in itself, it did pay its own way (anyone wishing to receive a catalogue had to send £1). It generated some direct sales and it generated some press interest in Jenga, off the back of which I was able to sell the game into a few more gift and toy stores.

Game Partners

At the end of 1982, the year after I left Intel, Sara Finch and Arabella Herschell also decided to leave the company in order to set up a business together. Sara was a professional designer, and their plan was to run a graphic design company catering specifically to the electronics industry, thereby capitalizing on their contacts within Intel.

Visiting me one evening for dinner in February 1983, they told me of their plans. At the time I had just found myself an office and warehouse to rent on a farm adjoining my mother's house a few miles outside Oxford.

"If you are looking for somewhere to work, how about subletting a corner of my office?" I suggested to Sara and Arabella. "Though I have to confess, it's probably a little grandiose of me to describe the building as an office. It's one of a series of WWII Nissen huts on a disused airstrip. For the past thirty years it's been used to house farm animals, pigs mostly. It isn't very glamorous, but it's incredibly cheap, and it has a loo, running water, and plenty of free parking."

"Sounds perfect, darling," Arabella purred. She did that. Purr, I mean. It was probably the effect of smoking Sobranie Black Russian cigarettes on an already naturally aristocratic and fruity voice.

"It's just what we need," Sara said.

So we moved in together. I placed one desk, a filing cabinet, and a phone at one end of the cavernous and very cold shed. At the other end, Sara and Arabella, with a large Persian rug, two desks, a filing cabinet, a phone, and a dog called Sherry, set up shop.

For the first few months of sharing the shed, Sara and Arabella carried on a business entirely separate from my own, but this changed when they showed me a game that a friend of Arabella had shown her. The game was based on the old Victorian game Word Making, Word Taking.

Sara and Arabella were considering devising a new game founded on this old idea and putting it on the market. They wondered if I might help. We played the game and I was instantly smitten and eager to lend a hand. It was, quite simply, the best and most competitive word game I had come across. The Victorian version of the game rather dully declared that it was "educational, enlightening, and informative." This totally missed the point that the game was extraordinarily competitive and challenging, and downright mean. And I mean, *mean.* Employing letter tiles, the game was comparable to Scrabble in some ways, as it involved building words. However—and this is what made it so interesting and exciting, unlike any other word game—it then permitted you to poach words from other players. I suggested it should be called "Swipe." The other two readily agreed, paid a visit to Mr. Jukes at Swann, Elt & Co., and quickly trademarked the word as the name of a game.

We then played the game many, many times to determine how many tiles of each letter of the alphabet should be included in a pack and the value each letter should be accorded. Sara designed a set of letter tiles. Printed on thick cardboard, the tiles were chevron-shaped and shiny black, front and back, with white lettering on one side. Each tile rather cleverly dovetailed into another. Adopting a packaging idea similar to the one I had used for Jenga, we had clear plastic sleeves made to snugly slip over a cardboard tray into which were stacked the letter tiles, the top ones spelling out the word SWIPE. The overall pack size was not much larger than a Mars Bar.

As mentioned, I advertised Swipe through The Loose Leaf Collection. I also added it to my product range, which meant that Leslie Scott Associates had officially become a *two*-product company. I felt this would give me greater credibility in the toy world, which it did, up to a point. Several stores that had previously ignored me agreed to stock both games, and some that were taking Jenga already were happy to add Swipe when they placed a new order.

Harrods, for example, agreed to stock Swipe with the proviso that I would demonstrate it along with Jenga in the store's adult games department for the whole of December in the run-up to Christmas. You can't really "demonstrate" Swipe the way you can Jenga, so I interpreted this request more loosely and had Sara make a static counter display and presentation that could stand alongside me, to which I could direct a prospective customer's attention.

Demonstrations and Terrorists

Harrods' adult games department is a lot more innocent than it sounds, selling nothing more risqué than bridge cards, chess, backgammon, and pastimes of that ilk. It was situated within the stationery department on the ground floor in front of the famous food hall, with men's apparel to the left and women's hosiery to the right. Aware that I couldn't afford to take the time every day for the entire month to demonstrate Jenga and Swipe in Harrods, I engaged two friends to help: Judith's elegant mother, Daphne Morgan, and a young student named Jane, whose last name I've embarrassingly now forgotten. Each of us would be there two days a week. As Sunday trading was forbidden at the time, I didn't have to worry about finding anyone to help me on the seventh day of the week.

When we started on December 1, Harrods' customers were already in the Christmas shopping mood, and we did a brisk trade. Anyone who stopped would invariably buy a copy of Jenga and many took a Swipe, too. Ten days later, when Christmas shopping had begun in earnest, Harrods was packed and our sales dropped. Although a dense crowd of potential customers swept up and down the aisle in front of our desk, they moved as a single unit. It was a brave individual who risked stopping to watch Jenga being played, because to do so caused a blockage that was easier for the crowd to shunt or push forward, or even mow down, than move around. Despite near-zero sales, the demonstrations had to go on. That had been my commitment.

On Saturday, December 17, I was supposed to be on demonstration duty all day, but just before one o'clock, I pushed against the crowd to make my way out of Harrods and walked a mile to a restaurant on the Fulham Road. It was a friend's birthday that day and my birthday was the next day, so I had arranged for Jane to demonstrate Jenga for a couple of hours so that I could slip away for a celebratory lunch.

Shortly before one-thirty the Irish Republican Army exploded a car bomb on Hans Crescent just outside Harrods at the entrance to men's apparel, starting what became the IRA's full-scale terror campaign in the heart of London. A mile away, at lunch and out of earshot, I knew nothing about any of this, and at around three o'clock, when I tried to get back to the store, it came as a complete surprise to find my route to Knightsbridge cordoned off. A young policeman manning the cordon told me that Harrods had been bombed and several people had been killed, including three police officers, one a particular friend of his, a woman police constable.

"She was only twenty-two years old. Just twenty-two. Twenty-two!" he kept repeating, the corners of his mouth pulled down as he tried hard to master his emotions and hold back the tears.

"I'm so sorry," I said. "This is awful. But, please. I need to get past. I need to get to Harrods. I need to find out if a young woman is safe. She's been working for me. Please. Please let me pass!"

He shook his head. "I can't. I'm sorry. I just can't. It's too dangerous. They think there may be another bomb. And in any case everyone has been moved already. The bomb exploded over an hour ago. So there's no point. She won't be there," he said in a gentle voice, pleading with me to be reasonable, and then adding more brusquely, "Please move along now. Go home. Ring her home. She will have rung home to tell everyone she is safe."

I realized then that my own family would have assumed I was in Harrods that day and that they would be desperate to hear from me, too.

In the days before mobile phones, the British post office's iconic red telephone boxes provided the only access to a phone outside the home or office. On a normal day they would be busy; on that particular day, there were impossibly long queues of people outside every red box I passed as I made my way to Paddington Station to catch the train home. There had been one box, I noticed with surprise, with a long queue made up exclusively of uniformed policemen and women. I assumed they were also ringing anxious family and friends.

Finally, in Paddington Station, I managed to get through to Jane's family to be told that though she was badly shaken—the stationery department had been showered in glass by the force of the blast—she was fine and on her way home. I then rang my mother to tell her I was safe and on my home.

Harrods was shut for three days. On December 20 it opened its doors again, and I went back to demonstrate Jenga. Given the fact that the IRA had threatened further bomb attacks in London, it was remarkable that so many Christmas shoppers returned to the store. Now, in an almost palpable air of defiance and bravado, the crowds moved more slowly and many people stopped and lingered at my stand and either played or good-humoredly encouraged others as they played. For people so famously undemonstrative and reserved as the British are, there was a notable demonstration of camaraderie and fun, with much laughter and oohs and aahs as the tower grew higher, and many gasps when it crashed. Each time it fell, players and audience happily scurried around helping to pick up the pieces. Most waited to watch me reassemble the tower to be ready for a new game before moving on.

Perhaps by collaborating in this simple building game, they were quietly expressing a desire to stand united against a force they felt was trying to bring down their way of life.

I sold a great many games in those five days before Christmas.

TEN

The Great and the Good

In the spring of 1984, having enjoyed working with Sara and Arabella on Swipe, I approached them with an idea I had for a magazine sparked by my experience with the Loose Leaf Collection the previous year. It had struck me that while there were many small-scale designers, manufacturers, and artisans selling directly to consumers at craft fairs or via mail order, there were no impartial, editorial guides to the goods and services available by post other than the passing references made by the shopping editors of a number of newspapers.

Good Gift

There appeared to be an opening for a glossy, quarterly magazine dedicated to sourcing and testing interesting products that could be purchased by post. Such a magazine might, at the same time, provide another conduit for promoting and selling Jenga and Swipe. Sara and Arabella loved the idea, and we agreed to join forces and publish *Good*

Gift. I would be *the* editor and a researcher and a writer; Sara would be *the* art director and a researcher; and Arabella would be *the* publisher and provide much of the necessary funds. The fact that not one of the three of us had any experience in publishing, or journalism, or even shopping by post seemed not to bother us a jot. On the contrary, this appeared to spur us on.

Consequently, at the same time as attempting to keep up the momentum with Jenga and Swipe (my 1984 diary is full of appointments with retail buyers up and down the country), I started working with Sara and Arabella to put together a dummy of our magazine, *Good Gift: An Editorial Guide to Shopping by Post*. I had discovered that to get a magazine onto the shelves of newsagents, you had first to sell the idea to a distribution company, the biggest of which was, and still is, one called Comag. I made an appointment to see an account executive at Comag and went down to London with the *Good Gift* dummy in my hand to make my pitch.

Eager to present and sell my idea, I had first to wait patiently as the account executive delivered a discouraging lecture on the inner workings of the industry. This, clearly, was intended to put me off.

"The consumer magazine market consists of thirty-five hundred titles, give or take a few, and competition is fierce."

"But there isn't a single magazine doing what we plan to do, so as far as I can see, we'll have no competitors."

"That's not quite how it will work. You will be competing with every single magazine published for women. Few women will buy a new specialist magazine in addition to their regular general magazine."

"Really?"

"Indeed," he said and carried on with his prepared speech.

"The magazine distribution chain in the UK comprises five levels in this order: publisher, distributor, wholesaler, retailer, and consumer. And all but the consumer take a share of the cover price for every copy sold."

"That's worse even than the toy trade," I interjected. "The poor author and publisher take all the risks and end up with just a tiny fraction from a sale!"

"Quite so." He nodded, pleased that I seemed to have grasped that point. "Comag physically moves the magazines to its network of appointed wholesalers around the country, each of which supplies the magazines to retailers within their designated geographical area."

Of the estimated fifty-five thousand retail outlets in the country, some six thousand–plus are owned by retail multiple chains, such as supermarkets, with the remainder independently owned. While the chains account for approximately 50 percent of total copy sales, independent retailers such as your local newsagent continue to account for about a third of all magazine sales."

"Who tells the retailers about the existence of a new magazine?"

"We do. The publisher has to be prepared to supply us with a minimum print run of sixty thousand copies of a magazine. The shops agree to put the magazine on their shelves for a specific period of time, one week for weeklies, one month for monthlies or quarterlies. After the agreed period of time, the shops bundle up and return any unsold copies to us, having clipped the corner of the front cover of every copy. We then invoice them for the copies sold."

"What do you do with the returns?"

"Shred them."

"*Shred* them, why?"

"That's how the system works."

"It's seems a dreadful waste. So. When do we see any money?"

"Approximately two months after we take delivery of the magazine, we will have sales figures and will pay you any money due."

"So we print sixty thousand copies of a magazine and have no idea how many sell and how many will be shredded until two months later?"

"Correct."

"Can you give us a worst-case/best-case estimate?"

"Yes. The worst case is that none are sold and sixty thousand are shredded; best case is that all are sold and none are shredded."

"The risk is entirely ours?"

"Correct."

"Blimey."

"Shall I take a look at the dummy?"

"Yes, please."

He looked at the dummy and told me he liked the basic idea, but our front cover needed to be considerably bolder.

"Do you think it will sell?"

"It might."

"Are you prepared to try it?"

"Are you prepared to provide us with sixty thousand copies?"

"Yes."

"Then we will be prepared to try it on the understanding that you beef up the front cover along the lines I have suggested."

"If October is your cover date, the magazine will need to be out to the newsagents by mid-September, so you will need to show me your final dummy in mid-July."

I returned to the office surprisingly (stupidly?) undaunted by the risks I now knew were involved. In fact, on the contrary, I was feeling triumphant that Comag had accepted the magazine. Convinced by my enthusiasm for the project, Arabella agreed to help fund production of the magazine, and work on our first edition began in earnest.

In addition to our own efforts, we commissioned articles from a number of friends, many of whom have gone on to become established writers, publishers, or critics and have probably long forgotten the contributions they made to our fledgling publication: Max Eilenberg, one-time publisher at Secker and Warburg and now a children's author; Susan Hitch, a broadcaster, critic, and academic; Jerome Fletcher, author and director of performance writing at Dartington

College; Susanne Greenhalgh, a Shakespearean scholar of considerable renown; Giulia Giuffre, an Australian academic and novelist; and a host of others.

Given the still low-tech nature of publishing at that time, all text had to be typeset by an outside company. We then had to check the galley proofs, so named because in the days of hand-set type the printer would set the page into galleys, metal frames into which the type was laid and tightened into place. The galley proofs were proofread and edited and passed to and fro between the typesetters and ourselves several times before they were finally cut and pasted onto layout sheets by Sara. Black-and-white photographs and illustrations had to be screened and color work separated into four plates: cyan, magenta, yellow, and black. It was an immensely time-consuming, expensive, and arduous process, and I am amazed, astounded even, leafing through the magazine today, that we three, with a little help from our friends, managed to produce the quality, almost slick, publication that *Good Gift* turned out to be.

That it was ever published at all is pretty amazing, too. On Friday, July 13, I traveled down to London with the final dummy to show to Comag, optimistically assuming that they would happily sign off on it and we would go to press a few weeks later. I was in for a nasty shock. The account executive told me that the major newsagents were not interested in stocking the magazine, so it wasn't worth Comag's time to take it, so it wasn't worth our time publishing it, either. I was flabbergasted.

"What reasons did they give for turning it down?" I asked when I found my voice.

"No reasons. They are not obliged to give any reasons."

"Well, what exactly did they say?"

"They said nothing."

"Well, how do you know they turned it down?"

"They didn't return the form ticking the box saying they wanted to take it."

"So you interpret no response as a negative response."

"Yes. Because it is, by default."

"Did they have any idea of what the magazine was about?"

"Of course, we sent a copy of your original dummy and a description to each one."

"No one from Comag presented the magazine in person?"

"No. We don't do that."

My mind was racing to find some way I could recover this situation.

"Would you give me the names and telephone numbers of the relevant buyers in W. H. Smith and Menzies?"

"Okay, but I warn you, they won't take your call, and they won't change their minds if they do."

"I can at least try. If I get them to agree to take the magazine, will you agree to distribute it as discussed?"

"Yes. But they won't. I'm sorry."

I left Comag and raced to the nearest phone box with a fistful of coins in my hand. If today I ever start to curse the now ubiquitous mobile phone, the memory of those frantic ten minutes I spent in that dank urine-smelling telephone box trying to rescue the magazine stops me dead, although the gods must have been on my side that day. I managed to wheedle my way past the W. H. Smith receptionist who answered my call, speak to the main buyer's secretary, and then to the man himself, who astonishingly agreed to see me later that day.

When I saw him, he told me that he had never seen the dummy, that it had, in all probability, been sifted out further down the selection procedure and had never made it to his desk. I explained the concept and showed him the final dummy I had with me. He said he liked the idea and he agreed to take it.

So, by the time I was in the train and on my way home, *Good Gift* was back on track.

In retrospect, Arabella may not consider that episode the lucky break that I did, for although we built up a decent and loyal circulation over its lifetime and covered some of our production costs by selling advertising space, the magazine lost money—a fair amount of money, and a sizable chunk of it Arabella's. We were forced to stop publishing after the third edition.

I realize now that although *Good Gift* was losing money when we shut it down, it is very likely that the goodwill we had built up in the title was worth as much, if not considerably more, than the amount we had invested in the project and accepted as lost. If we had made a concerted effort to sell *Good Gift* as a going concern, we would have found a buyer, of that I am now quite sure. *Good Gift* had shown that there was a demand in this busy market for this particular new title. It had muscled its way between the heavyweight titles to secure shelf space in the retail stores, an achievement that I now appreciate is akin to a new airline managing to acquire a landing slot at Heathrow, London's incredibly busy airport.

From lack of experience, and thus undaunted, we had had the confidence to create the magazine in the first place. From lack of experience, and thus cowed, we lost faith in the project and let *Good Gift* go without a trace except the holes it left in Arabella's and my own pockets.

Over the years, I have had time to reflect on the wisdom of turning to friends and family for financial support when embarking on a business venture. Having done this myself repeatedly, I now strongly advise against it when possible. It is very difficult to impose a firewall around a friendship sufficiently robust to protect the friendship from the damage, often beyond repair, that will be inflicted upon it should your business fail or even falter.

It's almost inevitable that friends or relatives who have invested in a venture that you proposed, which then fails, will feel let down and will believe, to some degree, that the project was oversold to them in the first place. It's a very human reaction to shift responsibility rather than face the truth that, in funding a project, you will be as liable for the success of that project as the person you have backed.

For an entrepreneur eager to get a project off the ground, it is easy, especially as a novice in a particular field, to skip over the finer details and end up convincing yourself of the very likely success of an enterprise. And once you have convinced yourself, you are more likely to be able to convince others to support you. The problem is that anyone's unqualified willingness to support your venture may convince you still further of the validity of your ideas. Friends or family generously and uncritically accepting your ideas at face value, warts and all, may not be doing you the greatest favor if, as a result, you don't closely examine your ideas for flaws. In this instance, the giver and the receiver may be well-advised to check a gift horse in the mouth, together.

I'm not sure if the enthusiasm and excitement I felt about all my various enterprises wasn't at times mistaken by others as supreme self-belief or a total absence of self-doubt. This might explain in part why Jerome and my mother and Arabella supported my ventures with a confidence I'm not always sure I felt myself. I say "in part" because I think in each case they had their own motives for getting involved, too—motives too individual and complex to try and explore too deeply here.

Suffice it to say, I think Jerome and my mother lent me money to help me realize my vision, and neither of them considered themselves business partners in the ventures they helped me fund. They were happy to assume that I would repay my debts sometime, sooner or later, although I'm sure they had both hoped it would be much sooner than it was.

In Arabella's case, although *Good Gift* was my idea, publishing it was a joint venture; at least that is how it began. The three of us were each to be as involved as the others in the production process. As it happened, the composition and publication of the magazine coincided with Arabella's meeting John Kiszley, getting married, and being swept off by her husband to an overseas posting with the army, which meant that she dropped out of all day-to-day involvement in the business. Yet still believing in the magazine's potential and genuinely concerned not to let us down, Arabella compensated (overcompensated, possibly) for her lack of direct involvement by continuing to fund LSA Publications, keeping it alive well beyond the moment when we all should have faced reality, accepted it was no longer viable, and shut it down or sold it. Arabella's financial investment in the project was lost when we finally closed down LSA Publications.

While we have remained amicably in touch over the intervening years, I am sure that her financial loss must have cast a shadow over our friendship. Researching this book, I had lunch with Arabella, now Lady Kiszley, in her beautiful country home in Gloucestershire where she and John have raised three boys and countless dogs and where her reputation as an artist steadily grows. After several glasses of red wine, I plucked up courage and asked Arabella what she had felt about *Good Gift*, LSA Publications, and all that. I was glad I did so. It was a relief to finally clear the air and hear that although she had experienced some regret, she had in the main been proud to have been associated with a magazine she believed should have worked. What's more, she believed still that *Good Gift* would have worked if we had all been more experienced and had had a proper business plan with proper milestones and an exit strategy—for example, a plan to sell the title to a major publisher at its zenith rather than allowing it to fade away.

Entering into joint business ventures with friends is tricky—more tricky than just borrowing or lending money to each other outright. For, however well you may think you know each other, and however frank your discussions have been about what you expect of one another, there will be assumptions on both sides that are not articulated precisely because you are friends.

Nevertheless, when you are starting out on your own with little or no track record, your family and friends, rather than the banks, are often the only ones who will be prepared to back you and give you a leg up.

Frederick Douglass, the first African-American to run for vice president (in 1872, on the Equal Rights Party ticket with Victoria Woodhull, the first woman to run for president), said in his speech, "Self-made Men," a speech that he gave many times: "It must in truth be said though it may not accord well with self-conscious individuality and self-conceit, that no possible native force of character, and no depth or wealth of originality, can lift a man into absolute independence of his fellow-man" (Frederick Douglass Papers, Library of Congress, undated).

Realistically, therefore, it is highly likely that an entrepreneur will at some early stage in her career call on a friend or two for financial help. A word of advice: Whatever might be the motives of your friends and however desperately you might need their help, always draw up a business plan with a disinterested third party present. If you cannot afford a lawyer, at least get someone who will probe behind the screen of politeness that exists between friends to ask and have answered all those necessary awkward questions, so as to ensure from the outset that you understand your respective commitments and expectations. People will still feel let down by you if the project fails, but you will find it easier to forgive yourself.

Some years later, I was amused to discover that Past Times, a new mail-order company at the time we were publishing *Good Gift*, had tried unsuccessfully to have its products reviewed in our magazine. Apparently, everything they had sent in for review had been returned, politely but firmly rejected as not meeting the magazine's exacting standards. Past Times became a fantastically successful mail-order gift business across the globe and opened a chain of stores throughout Britain. As it happened, it also became our biggest and most important customer some time after the magazine died and Sara and I had founded Oxford Games Ltd., designing and selling games for the gift market. I like to think that the games we designed exclusively for Past Times would have been accepted as meeting the exacting standards of those picky editors of *Good Gift*!

The Great Western Railway

I had to check and double-check my 1984 diary before I could accept that in October of that year, while I was working flat out on selling Jenga and Swipe, researching and writing copy for the spring issue of *Good Gift*, and still representing the National Theatre (popping down to London one night a week), Sara and I started work on our first commission to design a game.

In 1984, the then manager of Paddington Station, Richard Morris, contacted me to tell me that he loved the game Swipe (so much so that he had named his cat Swipe) and wondered if I might be interested in designing and producing a game to commemorate the 150th anniversary of the Great Western Railway coming up the following year.

I had always enjoyed traveling by train. And of course, having been at boarding school in the West Country, I knew about Isambard Kingdom Brunel, the famously audacious engineer who had built the West Country's railway network, tunnels, and bridges. Still, I was entirely unaware, until Richard pointed it out, that there was a huge body of people, mainly men and boys, who were passionately interested in the history of rail and the Great Western Railway in particular. The GWR, he informed me, was fondly known by its many admirers as God's Wonderful Railway. Enough said; of course I was interested in designing a GWR game.

A week later Sara and I took the train from Oxford to Paddington Station to meet and discuss this project with Richard over a cup of coffee in his office. He explained that while he could provide us with all the historical information and material we might need, and he could provide us with plenty of opportunities to promote the game when it came out, British Rail couldn't actually commission us to design the game or pay for the game to be published.

What strikes me as extraordinary now is that this didn't strike me as a problem at the time, and what is more extraordinary, it wasn't.

Back in Oxford, after the meeting, I rang the manager of Gibson Games Ltd., the family-owned games company that published 22b Baker Street (a game about Sherlock Holmes) and Diplomacy, my favorite board game of all time, and others. I introduced myself and told him that my partner and I had been asked to design a game for the GWR, and as I really liked the games Gibson published, I wanted to offer them the unique opportunity to publish our game. He thanked me and told me that they would—and they did—and that was that. The Great Western Railway Game was released in 1985 and is still traded on eBay today.

Some time later, I realized that it was not only exceedingly unusual for any games company to take on an untried and untested new game but also totally unheard of for any to agree to publish a game that was still to be designed by an unknown designer. I learned one very useful lesson from this experience, which I was to use many times. When my own name wouldn't open doors, I found it paid to align myself with an organization with name recognition strong enough to do it for me. And here I am, doing this again with this book. On this occasion, though, at least I can claim that I gave the more famous Jenga its name.

Now, let's return to that meeting at Paddington Station. Having finished our coffee, Richard asked if we wanted to have a look around the GWR's archives on a fact-finding mission to get inspiration for the game.

"Absolutely!" we both said.

"Well, at present, though none of the material is particularly well organized, it's all kept in a warehouse that's about half a mile down track number one.

"We could drive round by road, or given that there are no trains time-tabled to use that rail line this morning, it would be quicker to walk to the warehouse along the track."

"Fine," I said. "Let's do that."

Five minutes later, having donned enormously oversized fluorescent yellow jackets and huge yellow hard hats and gigantic steel-toed boots, Sara and I clambered down off the end of Platform One and waddled behind Richard, keeping fingers firmly crossed that his time-table was correct and we wouldn't suddenly find ourselves confronted by a locomotive bearing down on us at great speed.

We reached the warehouse unscathed, and a small, disconcertingly pallid elderly man who looked as though he hadn't seen daylight for an inordinately long stretch of time answered Richard's knock on the huge barn-worthy door.

"This is Sam, the caretaker of our collection," Richard said. "Sam will look after you and show you around and will ring me when you're ready to come back."

"Thank you," we replied.

"Please, come this way," said Sam, leading us into a dusty room containing several long wooden benches on top of which, in no apparent order, various bits of paper and objects were piled high.

Sam dithered around us in a state of nervous excitement, repeatedly pushing his pebble-thick glasses up the bridge of his nose and mumbling to us as we worked our way through this room of pretty dull stuff, until, seemingly unable to contain himself any longer, he cried out suddenly and loudly, "Come, come! Follow me! This is where the real treasures lie!"

Following him, we found ourselves by an enormous, thick metal door, apparently the entrance to a huge vault. Sam hopped over the lintel and into the room beyond and eagerly beckoned us within, where we found ourselves in an astonishingly cavernous and window-less space lined with countless shelves containing what appeared to be thousands and thousands of scrolls.

"Look. Look," Sam urged, selecting at random one of the scrolls and taking it to a table where he carefully unrolled it for us to see.

And what we saw was amazing. There revealed in front of us was a large (approximately four feet by four feet) beautifully executed engineering line drawing of a detailed section of railway track; a magnificent work of art in itself.

"Wow," we both said. "That's absolutely wonderful."

"Isn't it? Isn't it?" Sam agreed. "Feel it. Isn't it wonderful?" he added, pinching a corner of the scroll and rubbing it almost greedily between fingers and thumb.

"Feel it?" we asked, exchanging a puzzled look, but we both did what we were told.

"It's waxed linen. Linen of the finest quality," he sighed, smoothing his hand across the surface of the drawing. Then, gesturing at the shelves around us, he said, "Look! Rolls and rolls of exquisite linen. It's really the most terrible waste."

"Waste?" Sara asked, as surprised as I.

"Yes. Yes, waste. Just imagine what we could do with it. If we just boiled off the wax it would make the most beautiful ladies' underwear. Don't you ladies agree?" his eyes rolled in ecstasy at the very thought.

Seeing my bewilderment and then growing mirth reflected in Sara's face, I said quickly, "Yes, well, I suppose it might. Certainly unusual. Mmm, yes, ladies' underwear."

"Pants in particular, don't you think?"

"Pants?" I could see Sara's shoulders beginning to heave in silent laughter. It was definitely time to leave.

And without waiting to ring Richard, we made our excuses and were out of the warehouse and clumping back up the line to the station as fast as our size-ten boots would take us.

Though we would have loved to see more of those scrolls, if only to make sure they were not boiled down and lost forever, we really didn't feel we could cope with being cooped up with Sam again. Luckily for us, we were able to undertake all further research for the game in the museum at Didcot, which was run by railway enthusiasts with a rather more orthodox view of the value of the collection of GWR memorabilia they had in their care.

THE HISTORY OF THE GREAT WESTERN RAILWAY, we discovered, is very rich indeed. In large part designed by the great Brunel, in its heyday the GWR comprised soaring viaducts, grand stations, and vast tunnels—among them the famous Box Tunnel, the longest railway tunnel in the world at the time. (There is an apocryphal story that Box Tunnel is so oriented that the rising sun shines all the way through it on Brunel's birthday.) Furthermore, there were twenty-three hundred miles of track, sixteen hundred locomotives, forty-eight thousand other vehicles, several ships, a couple of coal mines, a number of iconic hotels, a bus company, and even, at one stage, an airline.

It was tricky knowing how to encapsulate this all in one game. However, it struck me while going through the railway museum that from its inception, the GWR company focused on promoting a particular image of itself, exhibiting to an extraordinary degree considerable flair in what today we would definitely call "branding." Attention was paid to every single detail of its operation, from the people it employed, to the color of its locomotives, to the inscriptions on the cutlery it used in its dining cars. Everything and everybody contributed toward creating what was and still remains GWR's reputation for being the grandest, the most glamorous, and the best railway company in the world.

Observing this, I devised a game in which players "travel" around the GWR network of through, main, and country railway lines as it existed in 1930, collecting, swapping, and forfeiting cards as they move. Each card is illustrated with an example of one facet (e.g., a famous locomotive, a well-known person, a promotional poster, a grand station) that contributed to the powerful overall identity of the GWR.

In 1985 Gibson Games published the numbered anniversary edition of five thousand Great Western Railway games and has reprinted the game several times since. It's no longer in print, but a brisk trade in secondhand games seems to continue, and it now exists as an exhibit in the Didcot museum, which initially inspired its creation.

The Origin of Oxford Games

Some time after the publication of the GWR game, the head of foreign acquisitions of Oxford's Bodleian Library, Peter Snow—an old friend, who incidentally was another one of our illustrious guest writers for *Good Gift*—introduced me to the library's innovative head of marketing, Joanna Dodsworth. Joanna asked if I would be interested in designing a game for the library, and so began a long working relationship with the university and the Bodleian in particular.

Oxford University's Bodleian Library, which today owns some 12 million books and manuscripts, can trace its origins back almost seven hundred years to when it started in a small room, now a vestry, in St. Mary's Church on Oxford's High Street. Today, a significant number of books are kept in the university's one hundred subject-specific libraries scattered throughout Oxford and several repositories outside the city (including one in an old salt mine in Cheshire). The majority of the Bodleian's priceless and ever-expanding collection, however, is housed in one of three places: the same beautiful buildings in the heart of the city that the library claimed in the fifteenth century and augmented in the sixteenth and seventeenth; in the vast "New Bodleian," built in the 1930s, across the other side of Broad Street; or in a network of underground caverns.

Indeed, 60 percent of the books are stored underground in these so-called stacks that exist several stories below the old and the new library buildings and under the wide street that runs between them. Down there, in the bowels of the earth, a little railway connects the two. Most Oxonians, and many visitors, too, know of the existence of these stacks and have heard rumors of the interconnecting railway, but few will ever have had the opportunity to go down and see these subterranean stores for themselves. As a general rule, the only people allowed down there are the Bodleian members of staff who work there locating and sending books up to the readers above and refiling books that are sent down once they have been read. It's an immensely important job, if you think about it. If you were to misfile a book, it could be lost forever.

When seeking inspiration for that first Bodleian Library game, I was given the rare opportunity to go down into the stacks and wander about at will. It was an unforgettable experience. Nothing I had ever imagined had prepared me for the astonishing sight of so many books filling so many shelves lining room after room after room. It was, quite literally, a mine of information.

The game I devised for the Bodleian was intended to mimic the experience of being a research student at the university at the time. Today the library is fully computerized and you can find books by subject and key words. Back in 1985, the books in the collection were indexed in ledgers or on little cards —as they had been for hundreds and hundreds of years—by title, author, and date of publication. To access a book, you had to know the exact title, and the only way to know this was by coming across a reference to that book in another book. It struck me that academic research was much like a treasure hunt in which you first have to locate an object, which then gives you a clue to how to track the next object, and so on.

In the game, you were asked to track down a number of books (fifteen, I seem to recall) that were all "necessary" to complete your research project. You were given the first book, which made reference to a couple of other books, telling you in which of the libraries in Oxford it was located, either on open shelves or stored in the stacks below. The board was a stylized map of Oxford depicting a dozen or more of the different libraries that make up the Bodleian, and you had to throw a die to move around. Once in the correct library, you could call up the "book" you sought (i.e., a card depicting the book), check it out, and find the reference it gave to another book or books you needed to complete your set.

As I wanted the Bodleian game to replicate as closely as possible the experience of using the Bodleian library, I spent several months "researching" the dozen or so research topics included in the game. Thus, all the books represented on cards, and all the references to which each referred, were genuine, as were some of the problems readers encountered in obtaining books they needed.

Unless a book was located on an open shelf in a library, the method for obtaining it was to fill in a pink request slip and wait for it to make its way, with countless others, to the out-of-town repository or through the in-house system to the stacks, where someone had to locate the book you wanted and send it back. It was usual for this process to take several hours, occasionally even a day or two, but much more often than not the system triumphed and the book you requested would appear. However, from time to time, rather than the book itself, you would receive the pink form with a white form attached explaining why the book wasn't there.

"Already out on loan" was the most frequent explanation, which was fair enough. "Temporarily mislaid" was a little more worrying, as clearly this meant "misfiled" and the temporary nature of the matter was therefore wishful thinking. But "destroyed in [the] Second World War" was definitely the most intriguing justification for one book I requested that hadn't even been published until 1963!

The Bodleian launched the game as a limited edition of twenty-five hundred, which they advertised to university alumni and sold to raise funds for the library. I understand that as a fund-raiser, the game was a success: the library sold out. As a game, I'm not quite so sure how well it was received. I thought it worked well and was really quite fun, but a few years after it was published I came across a copy in the Oxfam bookshop (a thrift shop), its outer shrink-wrap still intact. Clearly the game had never even been played, which disappointed me until my husband, a devotee of all thrift shops, Oxfam in particular, kindly suggested it must have been dearly cherished to have been donated to Oxfam in this pristine condition.

The Bodleian Game, published by the library itself, was printed and packaged by the same printers we had used to print and bind *Good Gift*. The next game we undertook for the university, The Hieroglyphs Game for the Ashmolean Museum, was the first game Sara and I published, packaged, and marketed under our own label, Finch & Scott, which later became Oxford Games Ltd.

ELEVEN

The Rise and Rise of Jenga

Throughout 1983 and '84 and much of '85, numerous activities that may now appear peripheral kept me busy, yet at the center of it all remained my driving ambition to get Jenga not only out but also about. Anybody given the chance to play the game loved it. I knew that the key to Jenga's potential success lay in giving people the opportunity to play the game or at the very least see it in play. However exciting the packaging, it was and still is difficult to grasp the appeal of Jenga without seeing it in motion.

To this end, I organized demonstrations of Jenga when and where possible. In April 1983, I was able to persuade *The Oxford Times* to sponsor the first-ever Jenga championship, which took place in the ballroom of the Randolph Hotel. The Randolph, standing across the street from the Ashmolean Museum, is the grandest of the old Oxford hotels, and it has been immortalized the TV series *Inspector Morse*, based on Colin Dexter's popular crime novels. In this magnificent setting, the Jenga championship drew a good crowd and considerable local media coverage, not only by *The Oxford Times* itself but also by local radio and television. Central

Television News ran a short but significant piece about the championship, about me, and about the game on the actual day of the event. Although this didn't exactly set the world on fire, it proved to be very helpful when it came to trying to sell the game into local stores. It also gave rise to the odd uncomfortable encounter or two.

"You're that bird that was on telly last night playing with them bricks, ain't you?" a gangly youth filling my car with petrol demanded.

"Um. Yes, yes. You're quite right, that was me."

"Ha! Bricks! Wha' ever next?! Ha, ha, ha. Ha, ha, ha."

"Ah, yes. Whatever indeed. Ha?"

For months to come, every time I went into that petrol station, this same young man would point at me, wink, and shout, "It's the brickie lady. Ha . . . bricks . . . ha, ha. Lady brick builder. Ha, ha, ha, ha."

I would laugh along with him, though I'm not sure I ever knew quite what I was laughing about and was, frankly, a little relieved when he left that job and I no longer had to run the gauntlet of these peculiar taunts every time I topped up my tank.

This particular youth aside, the majority of people seeing Jenga in action immediately grasped that, although only "wooden bricks," it would be a fun game to play.

Robert had a similar experience when he came to trying to sell the game in Canada. He also found that Jenga had to be demonstrated to create any impact. In his case, though, rather than impressing a gas station forecourt attendant, he was fortunate enough to catch the eye of a toy-industry maven, Hal Ross.

In February 1985, encouraged by my tale of *The Oxford Times* Randolph Hotel success, Robert arranged a Jenga tournament in the Cavendish Mall in Montreal, which was well attended and well covered by local and national press. Building on this positive response, Robert approached the toy merchandising manager at Zellers, a major department store chain with stores throughout Canada. The buyer loved Jenga and showed it to Hal Ross, then a salesman at Irwin Toy.

I now understand that it was Hal who took my original Jenga game to Irwin Toy and thus started the sequence of events that led to my assigning rights in the game to Robert, Robert to Pokonobe Associates, Pokonobe Associates to Irwin Toy, and Irwin Toy to Hasbro, which publishes and sells Jenga today.

Earlier this year, on a visit to the 2009 New York Toy Fair, I met up with Hal and his wife, Francine, and over a drink he told me this story.

"My dream of making it in the music business in New York was caving in on me when the Irwins offered me a job selling toys and games back home in Canada. I was very lucky. I discovered that not only did I love toys but that I was very good at selling them, too. Probably because buyers could sense that I was genuinely delighted with the products I sold.

"Anyway, one of the closest relationships I had in the toy business was with John Pritchard, who was merchandise manager of Zellers. He had been a buyer for another company when I and some others recommended him for this position that was opening up in Zellers. At that time, before Wal-Mart or Toys "R" Us came to Canada, Zellers was very, very important in the toy industry. So, sometime in early '85, I had a phone call from John who said, "I have just seen a game. You had better come down and see it. If you don't come down, I'm showing it to somebody else.

"So I flew down within a day or two, and the second he showed me Jenga, I flipped. I took the game back to the Irwins, and they, too, flipped at first glance. They all thought it was so great it had to be a winner—but the name! It bothered all of us, especially me. We argued about it for days.

"It didn't mean anything and we feared no one would be able to relate to it."

When I mentioned to Hal that I would have refused to let anyone change the name, even if they had wanted to do so, he laughed.

"Good for you!" he said, adding that at the time he had no idea that I had been there in the background tenaciously guarding the name. He, and everyone else at Irwin, had been under the impression that Pokonobe Associates had developed and owned this game. I told Hal that Pokonobe Associates had indeed *come* to own the game, but had had no part in creating or indeed developing it. In fact, as far as I was aware, it didn't even own the worldwide rights at the time Irwin was debating whether to hang on to the name.

I recounted for Hal and Francine a telephone conversation I had had with Robert the day he rang me to tell me Irwin was interested in Jenga, during which Robert had said something to the effect that they loved the game, but they hated the name Jenga: The Perpetual Challenge. "Irwin says Jenga means nothing and not many people will understand what perpetual means, either."

Robert had left me in no doubt that if I were to insist that Irwin keep my name for the game, Irwin might well choose to walk away from the deal—the deal for which I had already been persuaded was worth giving up my worldwide rights to Robert to enable him and his cousins to secure. Nevertheless, I stuck to my guns on this one point and insisted doggedly that if anyone wanted my game, they had to keep its name. Period. It had to be Jenga. I did, however, give way and allow *perpetual* to be replaced by *ultimate,* even though I felt very strongly that the former more accurately described the challenge that Jenga has to offer.

Returning to his story, Hal said, "Well, whether or not we were told that we had no choice but to keep the name, the more we thought about it, the more we came to accept that the fact that no one knew what Jenga meant was the best part about it. The name was new and different and would stand out and in time would become synonymous with the game."

That's when we decided to go all out and emphasize its unusual name. Do you remember seeing our first advert? The one about the game with the strange name?"

I certainly do remember this television commercial, and I also remember that I thought it tackled exceedingly well the combined problems of introducing into Canada a hitherto unknown game that was dubbed with a hitherto unknown word as its name.

> Jenga Jenga J J J J Jenga
>
> You take a block from the bottom and you put in on top,
>
> You take a block from the middle and you put it on the top
>
> It weebles and it wobbles but you just don't stop . . .

I don't recollect every word, but I remember that on screen a close-up of a game of Jenga would be unfolding as this jingle was chanted until, silenced by the tower collapsing with a mighty crash, a brief pause for effect was followed by the rallying cry:-

> . . . *JENGA, the grrreat game with the straaange name!*

On January 24, 1986, I flew to Canada to meet Robert for the first time and to attend the Toronto Toy Fair in order to witness Irwin Toy's triumphant relaunch of Jenga. Four years previously the Canadian inventors of Trivial Pursuit had debuted their game at this fair where it had been either totally ignored by the majority of the toy trade or actively dismissed as a nonstarter by the rest. In 1982, video games had just hit the market with a bang, and many believed that they would totally supersede any conventional board game. Who, they argued, would even want to play, let alone buy, an expensive game using an antiquated system of cards, counters, and boards? When, contrary to their expectations, Trivial Pursuit developed into a phenomenal global success, the Toronto Toy Fair became the experts' focus of attention for the next few years in their feverish hunt to identify and capture the next big thing. If the Canadians could do it once, they could do it again. And there are people who still think they did—with Jenga. One of the many myths surrounding the origin of the game is that its creator was Canadian, which is wrong. Although my father's mother was Canadian—and we do hold the deeds to one-third of a sheep island off the coast of Nova Scotia and a brownstone house in Quebec, but have been advised not to lay claim to either for fear of being hit with a hundred years's worth of back taxes—I am not Canadian. In fact, January 1986 was the first time that I set foot on Canadian soil or, to be more accurate, set foot on Canadian snow beneath which Canada's soil lay deeply, deeply buried.

The Sincerest Form of Flattery

Because the hotel and the exhibition center were interconnected, I spent my first forty-eight hours in Toronto quite happily living in a hermetically sealed environment, moving from my hotel room to the toy show without any need to step outside onto snow or soil. By Monday morning, however, this atmosphere had begun to pall. Feeling a little claustrophobic and in need of some fresh air, I went down to the lobby an hour before the show opened at nine, dressed in the old woolen duffel coat and scarf that saw me through winter in England.

I stepped outside briefly, only to rush back inside, shocked by the burning sensation of having my silver earrings painfully freeze in my earlobes. I later discovered that the temperature outside the hotel was an astonishing minus 30 degrees centigrade. It was the first time I had ever considered that England, which I had always found damp and cold, might appear, compared with other nations, to be one of those "warmer climes" that people often seek. Relieved that I had not lost any of my extremities to frostbite, I was back in position on the

Irwin booth by nine. As I had discovered the day before, in addition to introducing Jenga, Irwin was enthusiastically launching a new soft toy, Pound Puppies, "cute and adorable" little "orphaned" puppies that were to take over where the Cabbage Patch doll had just left off. Desperate to be given a good home, each of these little darlings came with an individual heartrending life history and, "just like real orphaned puppies everywhere," would start whining and barking hysterically if called or if anyone clapped his or her hands. Throughout the previous day, every time my demonstration game of Jenga had toppled and crashed (i.e., several times an hour), a thousand pounds of Pound Puppies would start up a sharp, yapping bark that severely jangled my nerves. I confess that barely an hour after I had arrived that Monday morning, by which time Jenga had crashed and set them off five or six times already, I had started to fantasize about the beautifully warm, supple coat and matching hat that could be made from a thousand Pound Puppy pelts. I kept this Cruella de Vil thought to myself.

Irwin Toy, the oldest and best-known toy company in Canada, was started by Sam Irwin in the 1920s, and his grandsons, George and Peter, were now involved in running this venerable business. By the time I arrived at the show in Canada I had had Jenga on the market for three years, time enough to realize that, on the whole, the toy trade is a remarkably joyless and serious affair run by men in suits, much like any other business where big money is at stake. It came as a pleasant surprise, therefore, to discover that behind the ubiquitous suits and serious air, the people selling fun at Irwin appeared to be genuinely fun people who enjoyed the toys and games they sold. Well, at least they *seemed* to enjoy playing my game with me, as well as having some fun at my expense. I'll explain.

I thought I had met all of the company's key people over the previous couple of days, so I was a little surprised when later that Monday morning a good-looking young man, sitting in a wheelchair with one of his legs in a cast, rolled up to me, smiled, extended his right hand

and said, "Hi, you must be Pokonobe's Jenga lady. I'm Peter Irwin, George's brother and head of marketing. Good to meet you."

"Yes, I'm Leslie Scott, the 'Jenga lady,' as you say. Good to meet you, too."

"Grrreat game," Peter said still smiling and raising his eyebrows a touch.

"With the straaange name?" I laughed, having watched the TV commercial many times since I had arrived in Canada.

"Umm, yes," he said slowly, shaking his head. "Indeed. That name's certainly going to be a challenge."

"Perpetual or ultimate?" I replied, then looking down at him, wondering if I had gone a little too far.

"Sorry?" he asked. "Ah, no. I see what you mean. Ha! Perpetual, I fear. But I'll be delighted to be proved wrong."

"You will be, I promise." I said. "Just give it time." Then, changing the subject, I asked, "What happened to your leg?"

"Oh, nothing much," he said. "I'll be out of this cast in a week or two."

Still curious, but unwilling to pry, I dropped the subject and asked, "I was just setting up the bricks—er, blocks—again. Would you like a quick game?"

"Thank you. I would, but later, perhaps? I need to catch Robert. Have you seen him?"

"He's walking around the show, I believe."

I watched Peter wheel himself away. A few minutes later, Robert appeared, looking a little agitated. Over the course of more than a year spent conducting business with Robert by phone, I had always assumed he would look and behave much like his three sisters. That is, that he would be casual and relaxed and have a mass of striking, red curly hair. I was surprised, when finally we met in person, to discover that Robert was dark-haired and rather dapper. More surprising still was to find that he had little of Gill's laissez-faire attitude toward life in general, and to me in particular. Quite the opposite, he seemed in an almost permanent state of anxiety that I might do or say something out of order that would let him down. I found this irritating and condescending, even mildly offensive, given that we were both there because of my game. But I did my level best to be quiet and behave.

"There's already a knockoff downstairs," Robert whispered.

"What do you mean?" I asked, finding myself whispering, too. "What's a knockoff?"

"Someone is showing a game that is almost a direct copy of Jenga," he replied, still whispering.

"Really? Who?" I asked, no longer quiet.

"Shh, shh, shh, shh," Robert said, indicating by tapping a finger to his lips that I should lower my voice. "A young guy who says a friend told him about a game he had seen last year when he visited London. He said it sounded like such a great idea, he made some himself and then decided to try it out at the toy show."

"He can't do that!" I shouted indignantly. "Can he?"

"No, of course not. I'm off to talk to Irwin right now."

For the next couple of hours, I continued to demonstrate the game, but I found it hard to concentrate. As I mentioned earlier, in 1982 I had been advised that my game was original enough to apply for a patent, I had held a patent pending for Jenga, until lack of funds had forced me to let my patent application lapse a couple of years later when faced with having to find the thousands and thousands of pounds I would need to take it any further. I had worried about the possibility of imitators but had convinced myself that trademarking the name and copyrighting the rules of play *would* provide adequate protection. It was one of the reasons I had been so insistent on Pokonobe Associates and Irwin Toy keeping the name. Hearing that someone may have copied the game concerned but did not unduly worry me. Nevertheless, I looked up anxiously when Robert reappeared.

"What did they have to say?" I pressed.

"They said they wanted to see you in room 467 on the fourth floor—straightaway," he replied.

"Oh, okay," I said, feeling a complex mixture of guilt and defiance very much as I used to feel on the many occasions I was summoned to see the headmistress at school.

I made my way up to the room Robert had told me to find and knocked.

"Come in," a rather gruff voice called out.

I walked in and found five men sitting along one side of a gleaming, French-polished table. Peter was one of them, parked sideways at the end of the row to accommodate his leg. I didn't recognize any of the other four, all dressed in nearly identical dark suits and wearing dark glasses, which I found rather disconcerting, if not a little threatening.

"Hello, Ms. Scott," Peter said, being oddly formal, I felt. "Thank you for coming up. Please take a seat."

The only spare chair was placed on the other side of the table from the men. I drew it out and sat down, feeling increasingly ill at ease. "Hello," I said. "You wanted to see me?"

"Yes, indeed," Peter said. "Has Robert told you why?"

"Well, he mentioned that someone was exhibiting a copy of Jenga. A *knock over* I think he called it."

"Off. A knock*off*. Have you seen it?"

"Yes. I popped downstairs to have a look before coming up here," I said. "There's a young guy who appears to have knocked out a few games himself. He told Robert a friend had shown him or told him about Jenga."

"That's what he told us, too," Peter said, and the four men nodded in solemn agreement.

"Well, he seems pretty harmless, but I guess he still needs to be told to stop trying to sell an imitation of Jenga. What will you do about it?"

I asked, looking first at Peter and then along the row, wondering why Peter had chosen not to introduce these other four men.

"The usual," Peter answered enigmatically.

"The usual?" I repeated. "What's the usual?"

"I don't think you want to know," one of the other men said in a low, chesty voice.

"I jolly well think I might," I replied in alarm and looked at Peter.

"Well, Bob or one of the others here," said Peter, nodding toward the men and continuing in a slow, slightly menacing tone, "will, er . . . deal with him."

"They'll do what?!" I gasped leaping to my feet. "You can't be—"

"It's how we do things here. How do you think I got this?" he said tapping his cast with a pen. No wonder he had evaded answering my question that morning.

"Good God! Please. You can't do this. It's too awful. It's ridiculous. I'm sure all you have to do is ask the guy to stop. He has no idea. He's very young . . ." I was appalled and terrified and very close to tears. It was only when I caught sight of a smile spreading from one man to another that it dawned on me that this had been an elaborate joke. They were all laughing quite openly now.

"I think that was an awful, awful thing to do," I said laughing with relief, but furious.

"Well, I'm not sure what I think about your willingness to believe we would do such a thing," Peter said.

"I don't know you! I've never been to Canada. I have no idea how you deal with each other over here!" I shouted in protest. "How could I know you were playing a game?"

That set them off laughing again, and this time I joined in, realizing that my gullibility had really been quite funny.

In the end I don't know what Irwin did say or do, but it was clearly intimidating enough. I don't believe I have seen that particular knockoff again. But there have been others, and today Jenga has the dubious honor of being copied frequently.

It is claimed that imitation is the sincerest form of flattery. If this is so, I would advocate in general heeding William Penn's advice and, when possible, "Avoid flatterers, for they are thieves in disguise." In the specific case of Jenga, I would add some stronger words of advice of my own. Jenga's current owners and publishers are very efficient (and effective) at identifying thieves disguised as flatterers. As they are apt to tenaciously protect their property, it would be best to avoid imitating the game of Jenga, under any guise.

Jenga Hits the Big Time

In February 2009, twenty-three years after Irwin first published and relaunched Jenga in Toronto, George Irwin recalled for me the events leading up to and following the 1986 show.

"We introduced Jenga at Toy Fair toward the end of January '86. Irwin Toy was lucky in that we wrote business at Toy Fair. We were one of the only companies that did. And I remember coming out of that fair on the third day with orders for close on eighty thousand pieces for the Canadian market. This was an unheard-of amount of business. That was as big as it gets. So we knew right then that we had a very good opportunity, a good game on our hands. As I recall, one of the things that made it happen was that we had a clever commercial that promoted Jenga as a great family game with a strange name.

"Anyway, there was a company called Schaper in Minneapolis. We distributed their product in Canada, and I called Bill Gerrity, then president of the company, and I said, 'We have this really incredible game called Jenga. You should introduce it at the New York Toy Fair in two weeks. We're going to do somewhere between eighty and a hundred thousand pieces in Canada, which means in the U.S. it should be somewhere between a million and a million two, which will make it an outstanding game.' And I said, 'You gotta take it.' So he said, 'What do you want for it?' and I said, 'We want a $50,000 advance,' and Bill said, 'That's a lot of money.' I said, 'I know, but I tell you, you're going to be a very, very happy guy because you got this deal.'

"Bill Gerrity was, you know, well, he was a legend. I was just in my thirties and Bill was in his sixties. He was my dad's age and he said, 'Okay, I'll take it,' without seeing it. He believed *me*, and he took it.

"The next day at Toy Fair, Alan Hassenfeld of Hasbro came through our booth and when he saw Jenga, he flipped. He said it was unbelievable. He asked how we were doing with it, and when I told him we're doing about eighty thousand pieces, he said, 'We've got to have it.' When I told him he couldn't because I had already done a deal with Schaper, he said, 'Why?! They're the wrong people. The game should be with Milton Bradley.' Hasbro had just bought Milton Bradley. I said, 'You know, Alan, I've made this deal with Bill Gerrity and that's the way it is.'

"So Alan went away. But two weeks later, the night before the New York Toy Show at which Schaper was about to launch the game—it was a Saturday night and I remember this very, very vividly—I get this phone call from Alan and he says, 'My brother Stephen [then president of Hasbro] and George Ditomassi [then president of Milton Bradley] and I want to come to talk to you about Jenga.' So I said okay and they came over to the hotel. It must have been some time around nine o'clock at night.

"For more than an hour we played Jenga, on our knees around a small coffee table in the middle of my hotel room. Finally, Stephen turned to me and said, 'We *need* to have this game,' and I said, 'You can't have it. I have to be good to my word. I've already promised it to Bill Gerrity. But if you like I can call Bill and ask if he is willing to give it to you.' So I called Bill and said, 'I'm sitting here with the Hassenfeld brothers and they want Jenga and are prepared to pay us fifty and you fifty to transfer it and take it and move it to their booth. Are you prepared to do it?' And he said no. I turned to the Hassenfelds who were right there and told them Bill had said no and they said offer him a hundred and fifty and Bill said no, so I hung up.

"Three months later Schaper got into financial trouble and Milton Bradley bought Schaper because of the game Jenga. And the rest is history."

George then corrected himself and said, "Actually, I think Tyco actually bought Schaper but part of the deal was that MB got Jenga and Tyco got some of the other games."

Rounding off our conversation, George said, "You know, Leslie, obviously Jenga was a turning point for you and clearly it was a turning point for the boys [Robert, Paul, and David of Pokonobe Associates]. Let's be honest, it took them down an unexpected path, and it made them a lot of money. But it was a turning point for us, too. I'm not sure you will ever understand the significance of what Jenga did for me personally or for our company, Irwin Toy.

"While they had always felt they knew a little about the toy business, my father and my uncle never really had the confidence to feel that we were good enough or smart enough to be able to find products ourselves and do it ourselves. And that had always frustrated me. Anyway, I managed to convince them we should do this product ourselves. So Jenga was the first product we did ourselves, and from that point on, we did a whole lot of product that followed the success of Jenga. If we had not done Jenga or if Jenga had been a failure, the whole company would likely have gone a different way. So the success of Jenga really launched us and gave us credibility as a company to be able to find product, to develop product, and to market product on a global basis."

Preparing to leave George in order to be shown around the Irwin Toy booth by Peter, I commented that, in view of what he had just told me, it seemed surprising that Irwin no longer published Jenga.

He explained that the Irwin family had decided to sell their company in 2000. Two years later, under new ownership, Irwin Toy went into bankruptcy and the company rights to publish Jenga reverted to Pokonobe Associates. Though George and Peter swiftly bought back the Irwin Toy name out of bankruptcy and restarted the family business, Pokonobe Associates had by then renegotiated the contract with Hasbro, granting them the license to publish the game, worldwide, including Canada.

George told me, "I think if there is one disappointment in my career, it is that Pokonobe did not give Jenga back to my brother Peter and me when we started Irwin Toy again. After doing what we did for everybody. After we had repackaged the game. And introduced the plastic sleeve that helped stack the game. And stamped Jenga into the bricks, literally branding the game. And found licensees for the game around the world. After all this, Pokonobe refused to give us the rights to publish the game, even in Canada, when we restarted our company."

Though it was clear that this was a situation that still irked him, George conceded with a small shrug, "I guess business is business. Pokonobe had Jenga and did with it what made the most business sense to them at the time."

Over at Hasbro, Alan Hassenfeld

Later that day, talking with Alan Hassenfeld, the chairman of Hasbro, I told him that I had visited Irwin's booth, where George had recounted his story of Jenga. I asked Alan if he could recollect when he first saw the game, and if he had ever been concerned about the name. This is his reply:

> From the moment I first saw it, I thought Jenga was an awesome game. I don't recall having any problem with the name. It already had traction.

So the issue of the name didn't come up, as far as I can remember. I think I saw it first in Toronto, but I vividly recall playing it with my brother Stevie, and George Irwin, who, outside Hasbro, is the best toy man in the business. He has a good nose. We were on our knees in some room in New York—my brother's flat maybe, or a hotel room—I don't recall. But I do remember we really, really wanted the game. And I remember Bill Gerrity—whom I highly, highly regarded—wouldn't give it over at the time. Later, when Schaper was in trouble, we wanted to buy some of their assets. And Jenga was definitely their best and most beautiful asset.

When asked, as I am from time to time, if I regret granting Pokonobe Associates the rights to Jenga, my answer is guarded. Partly it's because it is quite painful to face the fact that I might have made a mistake in giving away control of the game I created. It *is* the game that, though seemingly obvious to some, was extraordinary enough to have four Titans of the toy world on their knees playing it late into the night. Partly it's because, even though it was just "pure luck that they were fortunate enough to show it to the right guy," as Hal Ross believes, Robert did take Jenga to John Pritchard at Zellers and set off the chain of reactions that ultimately led to Jenga's becoming, under the Hasbro banner, one of the most popular games in the world, at times second only to Monopoly in global sales.

TWELVE

Gift-Wrapped Games

When I launched Jenga and followed it up with two other games, Swipe and the Great Western Railway Game, the toy market was the main, if not the only, outlet for games. Game designers and manufacturers exhibited their wares at toy fairs, and it was the buyers for dedicated toy stores or the toy buyers for department stores who had to be persuaded to stock a game. Jenga enjoyed a spectacular success in this environment once the market leaders, Irwin and Hasbro, had become its champions. The Great Western Railway Game published by Gibson Games succeeded in its own way, too. But quiet, understated, minimalist little Swipe, lacking the support of the big guns, didn't stand much of a chance even though it was (and is still) a veritable jewel of a word game.

In chapter 10 I described my attempts (before Irwin and then Milton Bradley swept up Jenga) to create a parallel market for Jenga and Swipe through a mail-order gift catalogue, The Loose Leaf Collection, and how this exercise led me on to publishing *Good Gift* magazine. Though neither of these endeavors was financially successful (on the contrary, *Good Gift* plunged me still deeper into debt), they provided the stimulus for a new venture that did finally make some money. Through Finch & Scott, which was to morph into Oxford Games Ltd., I devised and Sara illustrated games aimed specifically at the *gift*, rather than the *toy*, market.

The World of Gifts

When we first took games into the gift world, we found that we had the field pretty much to ourselves. Apart from a handful of businesses that included ornamental sets of classic games such as chess or back-gammon in their range of giftware, no producers designed games spe-cifically for the gift or book trade. We warily stepped out of the toy world and dipped our toes into the gift market by exhibiting at a tiny Museums' Association exhibition (a couple of stalls set up outside a conference room) with a prototype of The Hieroglyphs Game, which we had designed for Oxford's Ashmolean Museum.

Fortuitously for us, John Beale, the founder of the specialist toy store chain, The Early Learning Centre, was at that show. He had recently sold that company and had set up Historical Collections, which consisted of a new mail-order catalogue to be followed by the chain of high-end gift stores called Past Times. He, too, had moved away from toys into gifts.

"Watching people in museum gift stores, it occurred to me that they were not so much looking for souvenirs as for relics—not so much a memento of a nice day out as a vestige or piece of history," John told me when I asked him recently what had prompted him to start Past Times.

John expressed considerable interest in our game, which we planned to produce under our own label but with the endorsement of the Ashmolean Museum, for which we would pay the museum a royalty. We walked away from that tiny show with an order from Past Times and the conviction that the gift market was, without a doubt, where our future lay.

Using an analogy from the life of animals and plants, our effort to radiate into a new territory (i.e., the gift world) was successful because it coincided with a suitable "pollinator" moving into the same territory at precisely the same time. John Beale might not appreciate being likened to a pollinator, but in this context it really is quite apt if you are ready to accept the premise that the essence (the *idea*) of a plant is contained in its pollen. With The Hieroglyphs Game, we moved into the gift market with an original but historically themed game, just as John was looking for original products for his historically themed Past Times gift catalogue. John, attracted to our game because of its packaging, facilitated the propagation of our novel "species" of games just as a bee, attracted to a plant by its flower (its packaging), facilitates (albeit unwittingly) the propagation of a species of plant by transporting the plant's pollen from flower to flower.

As soon as The Hieroglyphs Game appeared in the Past Times catalogue, other gift catalogues and gift stores accepted in principle that suitably packaged games could be gift products, too.

Fewer than ten years after we launched The Hieroglyphs Game, the Oxford Games Collection comprised more than thirty games that we had designed and produced specifically for the gift market, several of which, like Ex Libris and Bookworm for the Bodleian, were endorsed by institutions that, in addition to selling the game through their own shops or catalogues, also received royalties from our sales of the games. For example, the Royal Shakespeare Company received royalties from Playing Shakespeare; the Royal Academy, the National Gallery, and the Tate received royalties from Retro; and Cambridge University's Fitzwilliam Museum received royalties from Inspiration.

In some instances, we designed and produced games on commission for organizations that wished to sell them under their own label;

for example, The Great Game of Comette, Auction, Hazard, and Six Victorian Parlour Games were games all exclusive to Past Times. Jammie Dodg'ems was exclusive to Burtons Biscuits; Thomas the Tank Engine to Marks & Spencer; the Islip Game and the Basel Game to the Islip Village Church and the Basel City Council, respectively. The Escape from the Temple of Laughter games were a collection of games designed to be included in the book of the same name by Jerome Fletcher and published by Scholastic Books.

As our reputation grew for designing games on commission, we found ourselves approached more and more frequently to consider some very strange ideas, most of which we rejected from the start. There are some issues that simply do not lend themselves as subjects for a game, at least not a game anyone would either buy or wish to play and therefore not a game I would wish to design. A game, after all, is supposed to be fun, which seems blindingly obvious to me but, as I found out, not to everybody else.

I was once asked in all seriousness to design a commercial game about HIV/AIDS to form part of an AIDS-awareness campaign. I declined. There are more appropriate ways of warning people against the dangers of unprotected sex and sharing needles, I think.

Less immediately obvious as a nonstarter was an idea presented to us by a Greek shipping magnate with a pied-à-terre in London. I don't now recall how he came to hear of us, but he invited Sara and me to dinner one evening to discuss a proposal for a game. Given our experience with one form of transport (i.e., rail) and assuming the game would have something to do with another (i.c., shipping), Sara and I thought this would be worth further exploration and accepted his invitation.

Dinner with him in his Holland Park house turned out to be an exceedingly odd affair. In a rather hot and overfurnished room during a lengthy and very heavy meal, our host lectured us not only about the Greek shipping business (which we had expected) but also about the terrible plight of Greek bears and turtles, which we had not expected, and he told us that he wanted to commission a game that combined all three topics. Before we had time to comment or ask questions, his attention was diverted (as was ours) by the exceptionally beautiful, languid young man who walked into the room, helped himself to a handful of pistachio nuts, and then walked out.

Turning back to us, sighing—but with no reference to this interruption—our host picked up where he had left off and continued excitedly to outline his idea for the game.

"Now. There are two things more ve must not forget," he said, offering us a plate of baklava and more sweet white wine.

"Two more problems Greece has to face that ve must address."

"In addition to saving bears and turtles?" I asked.

"Yes, in addition to ze bears and ze turtles. We have ze feral dogs."

"You want to save feral dogs?" I asked.

"Oh no, no. I vant to shot feral dogs. In fact, I vant to shot all dogs. Dogs are a filthy damn nuisance in Greece."

"Let me make sure I understand you. You want us to design a game about Greek shipping that involves saving Greek bears and Greek turtles and shooting feral Greek dogs?"

"Yes. That's correct, and other thing ve must not forget. Vital to Greek way of life. Boys must remember to obey their mothers—always!"

"I see. Yes, of course. Ships, bears, turtles, dogs, in addition to obedient sons."

At that point the beautiful man wandered in again, ignored us, smiled at our host, and wandered back out another door that led, we assumed, to the stairway that led to the bedrooms above, our host watching him all the while with a look of affection tinged with longing.

We took this as our cue to leave, and with profuse thanks for dinner and promises to think long and hard about this fascinating proposition, we hurried out into the night and beat a hasty retreat back to Oxford.

Mazes and Taverns

In addition to our endorsed and our exclusive games, in many cases, and more frequently as our range grew, we designed games for the Oxford Games Collection. The Game of Garden Maze, Tabula, The Celtic Knotwork (more a puzzle than a game), Old Money, Flummoxed, Inns & Taverns, Runestone, and many others all came about because in each case I or Sara was interested in the subject matter and thought there was potential for a game that might be intriguing and fun to play—and, most important, for which we believed there would be a market.

Perhaps a look at the concepts and inspiration for one or two might suffice to give a gist of the range of subjects we tackled. The Game of Maze capitalized on the revival of interest in the formal garden maze. After several years on the market, it had to be renamed "The Game of Garden Maze" when someone successfully trademarked the word *maze* for his game—another example of some of the odder decisions the Patent and Trademark Office has made over the years. The idea for this game was sparked off by meeting the maze designer Adrian Fisher at the opening of the hedge maze he had designed and planted at Leeds Castle. Adrian, now regarded as one of the greatest maze designers of all times, had with his partner Randoll Coate led the resurgence of interest in labyrinths and mazes that resulted in dozens of new hedge, stone, and even mirror mazes popping up in private homes and public spaces around the globe. Our maze game, played out on a board illustrated as a seventeenth-century formal garden, incorporated a short history of the labyrinth written for us by Adrian Fisher.

In another game, Inns & Taverns, we lightly touched on the cultural history of Britain as depicted by its pub signs. Signs outside taverns (*tabernae*) date back to Roman times. The naming of inns and public houses had become common in Britain by the twelfth century.

With pub names came pub signs bearing memorable images, since the majority of the population at that time could neither read nor write. The origin of many pub signs can be traced with ease. The Red Lion, for example, possibly the most common name for a pub, dates back to 1603 when James VI of Scotland became king of England, too (as James I), and ordered that the heraldic red lion of Scotland be displayed on all important buildings, including inns and taverns.

Other origins are wonderfully obscure, giving rise to amusing but not necessarily accurate speculation as to how they came about. For example, it has been suggested that London's famous "Elephant and Castle" is a corruption of *Infanta de Castile* (wife of Edward I) and the name of The Dog and Bacon, a pub in Horsham, is actually a distortion of "Dorking Beacon," a hill visible from the pub on a clear day. Nottingham's Ye Olde Trip to Jerusalem, established in 1189, claims the title of the oldest pub in England. It is believed that the name of the pub commemorates the crusaders who stopped for refreshments en route to the Holy Land. Incidentally, *trip* did not mean "journey" in Middle English (nor, I think, did it mean a hallucinatory experience induced by a psychedelic drug) but a resting place where such a journey could be broken from time to time.

IN SELECTING THE SUBJECT for a game, we had always to keep in mind our target market and avoid becoming too didactic. Appealing to an interest in a topic or fueling curiosity in one was okay; lecturing was not. Any hint that a game might be "educational" at the expense of its being challenging and enjoyable spelled the kiss of death for that game. Yet, equally important, having selected particular themes in order to attract interest beyond the usual market for games, we couldn't then disappoint by failing to impart some nuggets of information about that subject. It was a fine line to tread, and I'm not sure we always succeeded in keeping the balance just right. In playing

Runestone, for example, you might have learned all about the Elder Futhark, the runic alphabet (a subject I found fascinating), but I'm not sure the game was a great deal of fun.

There are authors one comes across from time to time (Richard Dawkins is one; Steven Pinker another) who write books about complex topics so skillfully that, even when the subject matter lies way outside your own area of expertise, the books are a pleasure to read and manage to make you, the reader, feel like a genius.

I have never had the skill to devise games that make anyone, least of all myself, feel like a genius, but I did strive with the Oxford Games Collection to create games that were a pleasure to play while either imparting some information or encouraging players to indulge and exhibit their own interests, creative talents, and ideas.

Ex Libris, for example, provides the material for play, but it is up to the players to use their imaginations and flex their literary muscles and pit their wits against each other. There are no right or wrong answers.

The upside of moving out of the highly competitive mainstream toy market was that we were able to adapt to a different environment by cultivating a subtler, quieter, and somewhat more sophisticated image for our games. In addition, encountering less competition meant that we could keep our advertising costs to a minimum and therefore could afford to sell smaller quantities into smaller, more exclusive mail-order catalogues and stores. Our products sold very successfully through such outlets. Being games and therefore unusual, they stood out on the shelf or the page, and, at the same time, because of the subject matter and the style and the design of their packaging, they sat well among collections of high-end quality giftware.

However, deliberately targeting the gift market resulted in limiting our games to this one very specific niche. Most of the games flourished in this environment and amply rewarded any investment in their creation. Some have even gone on to become classics in their own right

(Ex Libris and Anagram, in particular), but none has ever even begun to compare with the commercial success of Jenga.

A large part of this can be attributed to the fact that Jenga is, to borrow another concept from the natural world, a generalist. Being a generalist—as, for example, are the plants that gardeners accuse of being weeds—Jenga has managed to colonize, as weeds do, a wide range of very different territories simultaneously. Children like to play it, so it is available in toy stores. Teachers like to use it as a teaching aid, so it's available through educational suppliers. It is a popular adult drinking game, so you find it in pubs. Language is no barrier and neither is age, hence it can be perennially popular without acquiring craze status and is thus less likely to drop in and out of fashion as many other toys have done, such as the yo-yo and the hula hoop.

The flip side to such general success is that Jenga spawned a number of copies or knockoffs, some of which, like weeds themselves, rushed in to take advantage of the cleared space and perfect growing conditions Jenga created. Keeping the ground free of these imitations remains a challenge and, at the risk of taking this analogy a step too far, the most effective method of suppressing them has been to treat them like weeds and try to fill any gap in the market with an original Jenga game (or genuine Jenga line extension) as a gardener fills every space in a bed with desirable plants, leaving no room for weeds to take hold.

Creating a Brand

Ironically, one of the key reasons for Oxford Games's initial success in the gift market was to cause us the most problems in the long run. The upmarket gift market, much like the fashion industry, thrives on genuine novelty, or at least this is what many buyers have been taught to believe. If a product has been a resounding success one season, it risks being dropped from a range the next year precisely because it has been a success. Nothing frightens off the fashion-conscious faster than a sense that they may be late in latching on to the latest trend. However, judging whether a trend is still waxing or has begun to wane is notoriously tricky. Hence the rule of thumb, "Last year's success must be passé this year," tends to be applied.

As Malcolm Gladwell states in *The Tipping Point* (Little, Brown, 2000), fashion crazes, like the spread of disease, have the tendency to begin very slowly, taking incremental steps before they reach a critical mass and tip over into a full-scale epidemic. Leading, high-quality stores, such as Liberty's of London and Saks Fifth Avenue in New York, and boutique gift shops, too, like to consider themselves always slightly ahead of the field. For them the trick is to stock product at the beginning of a trend, taking it off the shelves just as sales reach the point of tipping over into mainstream fashion. These stores like to be seen as avant-garde, but they can't always afford to be too experimental.

It's a tricky business to get the timing just right, and rather than risk being caught with something considered ubiquitous, these stores often decide to withdraw earlier than might strictly be necessary. Profit margins frequently drive this strategy. While a product is popular but not freely available, elitist stores can charge a premium. However, even their most loyal customers are unlikely to pay over the odds when they know they, and what they might consider worse, *everyone else*, can buy the exact same product elsewhere.

So we found ourselves in the odd situation of having to design new games each year to satisfy the gift market's thirst for novelty, despite the fact that, as demonstrated by Scrabble, Monopoly, and Jenga, novelty is not what sells a game.

To tackle this problem, we made a conscious effort to create an image for the Oxford Games Collection as an entity in itself. We were hoping that those customers who had bought and enjoyed one of the games would assume, by implication, that the other games in the collection would be enjoyable, too. In other words, this time fully aware of what I was doing, I set out to brand Oxford Games.

I say "this time" because, although I would argue that today Jenga is a highly successful brand, or at the very least it is certainly a household name, anything that I did in its early history to facilitate the building of the brand *as distinct from the game* was done from an instinctive impulse rather than consciously planned. But, if this is the case, how and why did Jenga become such a successful brand?

Before attempting to answer this question, or even indeed *whether* it is the successful brand I claim it to be, I would like to explore what we mean when we talk about branding: namely what branding *is* and what branding *does*.

THIRTEEN

The Powerful Art of Branding

When you first arrive as a visitor to the Mpala Research Centre in Laikipia, Kenya, you are handed an information pack containing everything from an article on the history of Mpala (the forty-eight thousand-acre wildlife conservancy and working cattle ranch in which the centre is located) to logistics and security issues. It's a fat dossier; living and working in the middle of a huge tract of arid African bush land, where domestic livestock graze among wild animals, poses unique problems and real dangers that have to be managed with care. Part of this management relies on the time-honored tradition of branding.

Under the heading "Security and Movement," you will come across the following item as you read the Mpala Research Centre's visitors' information pack:

> Mpala cattle are branded—mostly with K2 and a lazy S below, are held in herds of approximately 120 head and, to protect them from preda-tion by lion, are kept in bomas (corrals) at night. If you see other brands on cattle herds or see any suspicious looking people, please report imme-diately either to the Head of Security or the Mpala Ranch Manager.

Do not confront the stock thieves or illegal grazers or poachers. They may be armed and can be aggressive.

So here, in northern Kenya, where cattle rustling is endemic (to the point where one might almost call it a game), you are left in no doubt about the purpose of branding, which is to clearly advertise ownership of your property (or products) and, more important, make sure there is absolutely no ambiguity about the message being signaled when that property is seen in a particular context. In this instance, only when the K2 and lazy S brand is sighted on cattle in a 120-strong herd should the signal be read as "Mpala cows being herded by Mpala staff—*hakuna matata* (no worries), it's safe to approach." In all other circumstances the message received must be *Hatari!*—"Flee and call security!"

However, just like anywhere else in the world, a cattle breeder's desire to indelibly mark his livestock goes further than making sure he can easily identify and, if necessary, reclaim any "lost" property. Among cattle cognoscenti, the provenance and therefore the likely value of an animal may be gleaned from reading its brand mark, provided, of course, it's an already known brand (i.e., it has been in existence long enough). This mark encapsulates both the quality of the animal and to some extent the reputation of its breeder (that is, of course, his reputation for raising animals with specific attributes).

For example, you don't have to spend much time among the cattle community in Laikipia to know that when you see a Mogwooni Ranch–branded bull, you can assume you are looking at a champion of the Boran breed, even if, like me, you know little about cattle and can't tell your Boran from your Brahmin. His reputation precedes him. The owners of Mogwooni have only ever bred Boran cattle from their own champion Boran bulls, so there is no reason to expect anything different of this one. Therefore, you can predict that he will be supremely well adapted to the arid conditions of the area, will be able to walk miles without flagging, will graze in the hottest sun, will put on weight in the worst drought, and will sire future champion Boran bulls and cows.

It could be argued, I think, that the concept of branding or, more specifically, brand marks being used *consciously* to signal ownership and differentiation as well as reputation, dates back to the Middle Ages with the adoption of heraldic coats of arms. To explain, let me take you on a slight detour and talk briefly about the history of heraldry (a fascinating subject I dipped into some years ago researching the game Tudor Joust).

Although symbolism and allegory, as seen in, for example, the eagle of the Roman legions and the Lion of Judah, have identified political entities throughout recorded history, *family* symbolism in the form of coats of arms is found only in Western Europe. (The Japanese *mon*, or family token, is, of course, comparable.) That these particular insignia, or brand marks, are *inheritable*, almost like physical traits that are passed down through families (e.g., a Roman nose or the Hapsburg chin), makes them particularly interesting. Like the brand mark on a Boran bull, they serve the functions of any brand mark: to visually and outwardly signal the hidden, or the less apparent, characteristics of the object being branded.

Today, scholars of the subject generally agree that heraldry and coats of arms applied to armor or woven into cloth banners probably came into active use during a time of war. This possibly happened during the Crusades, when the need arose for a quick way to identify an individual knight among otherwise indistinguishable knights dressed in armor massed on the field of battle. However, some believe that it was the institution of the tournament in the twelfth century that cemented the use of heraldry. During these mock battles, or war games, distinguishing one knight from another (for contestants and spectators alike) was as critical as it would be in warfare, but pageantry played a much greater part in them: the color and drama of heraldry would have added significantly to the visual splendor of the affair.

For the medieval European knights and for present-day Kenyan cattle, branding, like heraldry, is in essence the art of capturing and representing in a highly condensed form (whether by word or image or color) ownership, differentiation, and most important, reputation and character. You might say that a brand mark should reflect the true "nature of the beast" that it brands.

Today, if while out on a walk in Laikipia I come across a branded Mogwooni Ranch Boran bull, I know that I don't have to make a run for it and try to shimmy up the impossibly thorny trees that dot the Kenyan landscape. I recognize its brand. Boran bulls are known for their placid nature, despite their vast size. It would come as quite a shock if it did the unexpected, acted out of character, and decided to charge.

Back in the twelfth century, tournament knights, unlike Boran bulls, were expected to charge and do so with panache. I imagine much of the excitement of being a spectator at a game would have come from being able to identify and therefore ascertain the reputation and character of a contestant, a knight, by his coat of arms (his brand mark) and make an informed guess as to who would emerge as champion when two mounted knights in full armor charged at and tried to unseat each other with a lance.

Ironically, I had just finished writing these last few pages when I was confronted by my teenage daughter wanting to know if I would object to her getting a tattoo. In truth, I was appalled, but I am familiar enough with how my daughter ticks to know that if I were to express my disapproval, I would be as good as kicking her toward the nearest tattoo parlor. So I told her I needed a little time to think over this interesting idea and slipped off to do some hasty research and quiet reflection.

A few days later, I sat her down to explain. "Tattooing, that is, indelibly marking or branding human skin, has a very long history in many cultures of being used to signal the character of the tattooed. It should never be assumed to be simply decorative. In choosing to brand your own skin with a tattoo you are, by definition, making a statement about yourself.

"Are you certain you understand the language of tattoo? Did you know, for example, that in some criminal gangs the strands of the spider's web tattooed on your elbow indicates how many people you've killed? And even if you are confident that the message is clear, are you certain that this is what you will want to say about yourself for the rest of your life? After all, we are talking about something irreversible here, casting in concrete, carving in stone . . ."

"Bloody hell, Mum," she interrupted, laughing. "I'm hardly likely to be mistaken for a gangland hit man, even if I did get a spiderweb tattoo. Stop lecturing me."

"I'm not lecturing. I just want to make sure you understand the significance of what you are wanting to do."

And then I continued to lecture, probably ineffectually, because what I was trying to defend was probably an indefensible prejudice. I entertain an English middle-class, middle-aged mother's irrational feelings of mistrust of a practice I know little about but somehow instinctively associate with sailors, criminals, circus performers, and Hell's Angels.

I'm fully aware that my ideas about what tattoos signify in Western culture today may be a little out of date (*prehistoric*, my daughter would say), but I don't think I'm wrong when I suggest that they continue to do what branding has always done: to identify and represent something about the character of the product being branded. And because they do it in a manner that is difficult, if not impossible, to erase, I think everyone should be a little cautious about their use.

There is another method of personal branding in vogue with the young today that I think should also be handled with care, or at least with an eye to their personal futures, and this is the use of social networking websites such as MySpace and Facebook. Here, too, there is the strong likelihood that your perception of yourself and how you would like others to see you may alter with time, and here, too, it might be difficult or impossible to alter how you have chosen to brand yourself once you leave such an indelible mark in the ether.

But back now to some of the questions I posed at the end of the previous chapter. Jenga is certainly a successful product, but is Jenga a successful brand?

GIVEN THAT I BELIEVE a brand is something that captures and represents, in the highly condensed form of a word or an image, ownership, differentiation, character, and reputation, I think Jenga is a very successful brand—so successful that Jenga has become a concept that has taken on a life of its own way beyond the toy world into which the game was launched.

Today, Jenga crops up all over the place, from the anarchic cartoon show, *Family Guy* to articles in the serious scientific journal, *Nature*, usually employed as a metaphor for a particular type of instability. I think this may be because, essentially, it is a unique game and a unique word; Jenga the brand is *synonymous* with Jenga the game. The game and its name were born together and grew up together and are now inseparable. Hear the word or see the word and you think of the game. See the game and you think of the name. Not all brands succeed in achieving so close a link between the product being marketed and the image conveyed by a brand mark, perhaps because in many cases, branding happens the other way around. A word or image is chosen to brand a product because of the concept that the word or image already encapsulates, even when there is no cognitive relationship between product and word.

In fact, some very famous examples (Nike for one) exhibit so great a disconnect between the aura of the *brand* and the specific *product* it purports to identify as to suggest that some phenomenon subtly different from branding, at least as I have defined branding, may be going on. However, this use of the word *branding* to label what is in fact the marketing of ethereal ideas rather than tangible goods or services is so widespread that I think perhaps a clear distinction needs to be made between the two.

What distinguishes one type of branding (such as Jenga) from another (such as Nike) is that, even though both types may encapsulate and represent the reputation and the character of a product for sale, in the second case the product for sale is, first and foremost, the brand itself. Furthermore, I suggest that companies turn to this form of branding when there is nothing intrinsically unique about the products they sell.

For example, I would argue that because there appears to be little obvious difference between Nike's running shoes and those of its competitors, to differentiate itself from other shoe companies, Nike created and branded a myth. In ancient Greek mythology, Nike is the winged goddess of strength, speed, and victory. Clearly inspired by the goddess whose name it had adopted as its own, Nike the company set out to establish a mythical world, or society, inhabited by sports heroes (latter-day gods) such as Michael Jordan, in which ordinary mortals (well, mainly teenage boys) have the opportunity to strive for and win the crown, the victor's prize, the mark of sweet renown that only Nike can confer. In other words, when you buy Nike shoes, you don't just buy any old sweaty sneaker or trainer, you buy a passport to Nike's enchanted world. The only way of gaining access to that particular world, to that particular culture, is by owning and wearing Nike shoes. Nike defines, owns, and sells membership to the club.

This branding of a lifestyle is an astonishingly successful way to sell shoes and, as it turns out, thousands of other products that would be indistinguishable from one another if not for the brand logo they prominently display. Its success, however, rests almost entirely on a company's ability to keep persuading its customers to keep buying into whatever myth or yarn it continues to spin. Natural cynic that I am, I find it hard to believe that otherwise prosaic businesspeople truly believe all of the romantic tales they weave to sell their wares—the tales they want and need us to believe. Yet, I must assume that they either believe their own stories, or they are in fact telling the truth. For nothing is as effective in the business of persuasion as telling it like you mean it. Except, of course, actually *meaning* what you say.

Not all huge corporations have had to resort to building their brand's reputation on a myth. Hasbro, for example, has a huge portfolio of toys and games that includes numerous stand-alone brands: Transformers, G.I. Joe, Monopoly, Jenga—each brand with its story and its own character and reputation. The one thing they have in common is that each carries the Hasbro brand and therefore its "seal of approval." This guarantees that the product will live up to the Hasbro brand's reputation for quality. As the company's group executive, Phil Jackson, told me, "The consumer can be confident that a Hasbro toy or game will meet the highest standards of manufacturing in the industry." In the case of Jenga, this means that consumers can be certain that if they purchase a genuine Jenga game, rather than a knockoff, it will be made from "good wood." "The wood will come from certified sustainable forests. The wood will be 100 percent nontoxic. The wood will not splinter."

He added that "Alan Hassenfeld makes sure that Hasbro is a leader in social and environmental responsibilities. As a Hasbro-branded product, Jenga, you can be certain, will be made in factories where the health, safety, and welfare of the employees are of paramount importance."

Whether your brand is corporeal (a game of Jenga) or a figment of imagination (a lifestyle), living up to your reputation is the most powerful tool in the powerful art of branding.

FOURTEEN

But Is It Art?

In referring to branding as an art as I did in the previous chapter's title, I use the word *art* in the sense of a "skill" or "mastery" as, for example, one might refer to some cooking (not necessarily mine) as an art and a chef as an artist. I suggest that branding might be considered an art because, like all art, it uses artifacts or images with symbolic meanings as a method of communication. I am not, I hasten to add, attempting to elevate branding to the level of Art with a capital A, the kind of Art that, according to Germaine Greer, is so powerful it "enables the immortal soul to emancipate itself from the dying animal" (*The Guardian*, February 11, 2008) but to make the point that it is an art form as distinct from a science.

Developing a Brand

Science, rigorous science at least, is by definition the use of systematic observation and experimentation under controlled conditions to test hypotheses or presumptions. Key to the concept of science is that you should be able to repeat an experiment because you can control the environment in which you conduct that experiment. And from that you should, with a high degree of accuracy, be able to predict results.

You can't do this when branding a product because you are simply not at liberty to experiment within controlled conditions. You cannot, for example, blithely recreate the Great Depression of the 1930s to test the effect that another depression would have on the sales of a game. What you can do, though, is by extrapolation use historical or scientific facts to predict an outcome and so craft your brand to take advantage of a given environment or situation. To do this, and to do it well, as in all art, requires more than just access to facts or data. It requires an intimate knowledge of the mores and traditions—the culture—of the people you are addressing, and it requires intuition, imagination, creativity, and above all a command of the idiom of signing: of directly, through speech, or indirectly, through images and symbols, representing and communicating ideas.

Did I think of myself as an artist creating a work of art when I first devised and named Jenga? Was I in full command of the language of signing and consciously crafting a brand? Well, no, I can't truthfully say that I was.

With hindsight I can see that there were two key moments in the history of the game, aside from putting the game on the market in the first place, when I made marketing decisions perhaps as a result of an intuitive understanding of the art of branding. At those key moments I may have had an instinctive sense of what Jenga as a brand might become.

The first was when the Irwin people wanted to change its name and I refused to let them. The second was when, later, after Jenga's first flush of success, Hasbro considered bringing out a range of three-dimensional wooden games and puzzles under the Jenga name, and I begged the company not to.

I remember arguing quite vociferously, probably to the point of being rude, that it was clear that neither Pokonobe Associates' nor Hasbro's marketing people understood the essential appeal and therefore the success of the game if they were so ready to water down its image in this way. The fact that it was made of wood was certainly a factor in the game's success. But that was by no means *the* defining element, and calling any product a "Jenga game" or a "Jenga puzzle" solely because it was wood and expecting it to sell as a result struck me as entirely missing the point.

Luckily for "Brand Jenga," this idea was never pursued. Hasbro has published various line-extensions of the game over the years, from Throw 'n Go Jenga to Xtreme Jenga, and Pokonobe Associates recently sanctioned electronic versions of Jenga for Wii and Xbox, but in almost every instance the character of the game remains quintessentially the same —even, curiously, when played electronically by cyber-hands. Therefore, none yet have had the effect of weakening the Jenga brand. Indeed, some variations (the computer games in particular) may have even strengthened it.

The toy and gift industries are littered with examples of the costly mistakes that can happen in an effort to make the most of a successful brand. Typically, these arise when the expensive marketing guru employed to manage branding loses sight of the intrinsic personality of the product that has been branded.

LEGO

In 1995, I was invited to design a game for LEGO, the company known worldwide for its plastic building blocks. I assumed from the initial telephone conversation with the marketing people in the UK that LEGO was looking to capitalize on their image to branch into new markets, and that what they wanted from me was some sort of board game that somehow incorporated the iconic LEGO brick.

I devised and mocked up a board game that involved collecting and assembling LEGO pieces. It turned out that it wasn't what LEGO wanted at all, and they seemed rather puzzled that I had thought it might be. At that time, my family and I were living in Aarhus, Denmark, in the heart of LEGO country. The name "Lego" derives from the Danish *leg godt*, play well. My children, like all their Danish friends, were LEGO fanatics, and LEGO was certainly played "godt"—with great gusto—all over our home. Under these circumstances, it was neither puzzling that I felt that LEGO was synonymous with the plastic building brick I trod on or vacuumed up daily, nor odd that I couldn't imagine what image LEGO might build on if not their brick.

The company executive I spoke with explained that of course their core business would always be the brick and variations of it, but they had now decided it was time to diversify into other markets. They were planning to use LEGO's reputation for quality to "brand" other children's products. And then they showed me the range of children's clothes and shoes they were about to launch. I was very surprised that they were moving into clothing and even more surprised that there wasn't a single item in the range that seemed to have been inspired by their famous brick. To me, it looked like any other collection of shirts, skirts, and trousers for children and was, if anything, more subdued than most, not even capitalizing on the bright primary colors that I associated with the LEGO brick. They felt that it was enough to call the range the "LEGO Collection" to imbue the clothes with the appeal of the LEGO toys.

However, it didn't work that way. The clothing range flopped, and I think it did so because there was a serious flaw in the logic. No child self-conscious enough to care about the label of the brand of clothing he or she wears is likely to feel cool wearing LEGO, a brand so heavily associated with a children's toy. And adults buying clothes for children are unlikely to make the automatic assumption that LEGO clothes would be superior and therefore justifiably more expensive than any existing range of clothes for children, just because LEGO was known for making great plastic bricks.

This mistake didn't cripple Lego, but it certainly cost them dearly.

Having learned from this expensive experience, LEGO's managers returned to focusing on the company's core strengths. Today LEGO is now the seventh most powerful brand worldwide among families with children (how this is measured, I'm not sure) and so confident of its own image and what it calls its "LEGO values" that it feels justified in stating that "a brand without a personality is like a human without character: plain, boring, unnoticed." I assume the company is implying that the LEGO brand is none of these because it has bags of personality and therefore oodles of character. The exact nature of this personality and character is left somewhat vague, perhaps deliberately, given that "Just imagine . . ." is LEGO's new brand statement, replacing "Play on."

The idea that brands actually have personality and character is pretty similar to a point I made in the last chapter, where I discuss Boran bulls and medieval knights. Successful branding captures and portrays the *character* of the product it brands. This leads me to think that if branding is indeed an art, then perhaps it is the art of characterization, and therefore, there are techniques that might be learned from the masters of this art, such as cartoonists, novelists, playwrights, and actors, all of whom artfully control the impressions others form of the characters they create through vivid graphic or verbal description or performance. The best of these latter artists are able to portray their creations with such finesse that we, the audience, without time for much reflection, will understand the personality of the characters portrayed well enough to incorporate them into the overall narrative. I don't want to suggest that in order to brand a product well, you need the artistic sensibilities of a great playwright or actor, but I do believe that adopting some of their techniques of characterization can help. For example, having carefully crafted a believable character, a playwright would take care that this individual doesn't suddenly behave oddly and irrationally *out* of character, unless, of course, it is to highlight a particular point.

It takes considerable skill to build up the character of a brand to such a stage that your audience (i.e., your customers) are confident that they now know what to expect from your brand. It is only too easy to lose this trust if you don't employ an equal amount of skill in making sure the brand doesn't suddenly, irrationally, without plausible explanation, exhibit traits that are totally out of character.

Anyone who enjoys a game of Jenga would expect, with some justification, to find the same essential qualities of the original in any other game sold under the Jenga brand. I'm not sure I could have articulated, until very recently (in fact, until I started to write this book), the essential traits that define Jenga. But I had an instinctive idea that stacking any old thing on top of another until the whole structure falls would not be enough for a game to qualify as a "Jenga game," any more than fashioning a puzzle out of wood would merit its being called a "Jenga puzzle."

When Sara and I branded our range of games, the Oxford Games Collection, we justified the use of the word *Oxford* because we were based in Oxford, but in all honesty, we used it because of its connotations. That is, by hinting at an association with the world-famous university on our doorstep, we implied that we were offering pastimes that were to some degree more intellectual than most games. By calling the range a collection, we suggested that, though different from one another, the games all had this trait in common.

Presumptuous as it might have been for us to suggest that our products were somehow infused with an air of learning and sophistication, having deliberately built up this reputation, we knew each new game we added to that collection would have to remain in character. It would have been confusing if we had unexpectedly published some of our more frivolous ideas under this label. For example, Mutton: The Great Game of Sheep was a gloriously silly game we played privately using plastic model sheep. It amused us, but we would have perplexed our Oxford Games clients. Hence, we never marketed it.

The sociologist Erving Goffman, in his famous work *The Presentation of Self in Everyday Life* (Penguin Books, 1990), suggests that the expressiveness of an individual (and therefore his capacity to give impressions) appears to involve two radically different kinds of sign activity: the expression that he *gives* and the expression that he *gives off.* The first involves verbal symbols or their substitutes that are used to communicate information that he and others are known to attach to these symbols. The second involves less obvious, though equally important, signaling such as the setting, appearance, and manner by which others make inferences about his character. For a performance to be convincing, it requires coherence between what is actually stated (verbally or otherwise) and what is implied (by setting, appearance, and manner).

Of course, a mismatch between the expression *given* and the expression *given off* can be used deliberately to positive effect—in fiction, at least. In the classic television series *Columbo*, the character of Lieutenant Columbo is a shabby, apparently slow-witted police detective whose fumbling, overly polite manner belies his brilliance as a homicide investigator. Columbo deliberately uses a deferential and absentminded persona to lull criminal suspects into a false sense of security. Meanwhile, he solves his cases by paying close attention to tiny inconsistencies in a suspect's story and by relentlessly hounding suspects until they break down, either confessing to the crime or otherwise irrevocably revealing their guilt.

Now, whereas giving out mixed messages Columbo-style may work for a fictitious cop, it is a dangerous idea in real-life branding. To be effective in the long run, a brand should signal unambiguous information, and only that, about the character or the nature of the product it brands. Having set out to sell the idea that branding should be considered an art, I'm about to call on science, biology in particular, to elaborate, because the natural world is teeming with examples of some of the greatest salesmen on this planet: animals and plants that have evolved astonishingly effective ways of marketing and branding the products they have for sale.

Biological Branding

Biologists will tell you that the goal of any life form is to reproduce and pass on to subsequent generations as many of its genes as possible. Thus, all animal and plant behavior, however extraordinary or outlandish it might appear, should always be interpreted in the light of this overriding drive to reproduce. In order to fulfill its mission in life, a plant or an animal has to achieve all of the following:

1. Survive long enough to reach sexual maturity.
2. Successfully compete for and/or attract a mate.
3. Reproduce.
4. Ensure that its offspring reach maturity and pass on their genes to the next generation.

In striving to negotiate these stages, animals and plants have evolved myriad ingenious ways of packaging, protecting, and promoting (in other words, branding) the product each has for sale, namely itself, or more specifically, its unique packet of genes. From the very fact of its existence, it may be assumed that every living plant and creature is an expert in branding its own wares in its own particular environment (its marketplace). Perhaps, in studying the work of these masters of the art, we might learn of tried-and-tested techniques that could be borrowed and applied to our own mercantile affairs.

Take coral reef fish, for example. I've just returned from a week's snorkeling off the coast of Kenya, so a dazzling impression of these Technicolor creatures is still very fresh in my mind. But I wonder, why are these fish so variously shaped and so brightly colored?

Joe Levine, in "In Living Colors" (*Natural History*, September 1999), suggests the following: "The medium is the message among coral fishes. Their vivid colors and extraordinary shapes tell a thousand tales." He goes on to remind us that Konrad Lorenz, the Nobel Laureate and founder of modern ethology (the scientific study of animal behavior), was convinced that many coral reef fishes use their bodies as living billboards to advertise themselves. It was Lorenz who first coined the term *Plakatfarben* (poster colors), used today to describe brightly colored water-based paints. "Some fish," Lorenz said, "even do their advertising in the manner of electronic neon signs rather than static billboards and can alter their body colors at whim."

But why do these creatures need to be so visible and invest so much in advertising this way? The costs of producing these colors, in terms of the energy required and therefore the food and time spent foraging for this food, can be enormous because fish, like most animals, cannot synthesize color. They depend on different natural pigments (carotenoids mainly) in their diet to provide different colors. The brighter the hue, the more natural pigment is required. Most of these natural pigments are in limited supply, and as a result, they are costly in terms of energy for the fish to track down. The carotenoid required to make red, for example, is especially rare, and therefore particularly "expensive." But even yellow and blue don't come cheap. Consequently, I assume we can assume that if these fishes are prepared to "spend" so much to acquire these pigments, there must be significant benefits to promoting in color. In their case, full-color poster advertising must pay. But what is being promoted, and to whom?

Bearing in mind that the "product" each fish needs to sell is his or her package of genes, and individuals of either sex seek to maximize their total reproductive output during their lifetimes, it is fair to suggest that some or all of the following must apply:

- A fish signals its sex, fitness, and readiness to mate to potential mates (customers).
- A fish marks its territory and warns others (competitors) off its patch.
- A fish signals its fitness and ability to outswim others (predators) in a chase to avoid both wasting time and energy.

Of course, aside from coral reef fish, there are many other extraordinary and wonderful examples of animals that invest in spectacular advertising. The important issue of costs versus benefits associated with advertising in animals is revealing in the context of a discussion about human branding. And here I mean commercial product branding, not partner selection in humans. For example, what is going on in the case of an animal such as the male widow bird with its extravagantly long black tail? It is so long and so heavy that it would appear more of a burden than an asset; the poor bird can barely fly. Why is it literally weighed down with such enormous *advertising* costs? It makes little sense to conclude that what the bird is advertising for sale is its tail. This would be like suggesting that the famous "Flying Lady" (or Spirit of Ecstasy) mascot mounted on the hood of a Rolls Royce car is what Rolls Royce makes and sells. You don't buy a Rolls Royce car to acquire its mascot, even if (like me) it is by its mascot that you recognize the car as a Rolls Royce.

More likely, what one sees here in the case of the widow bird is an example of the evolutionary biologist Amotz Zahavi's "handicap principle" at work. The male bird is advertising to all nubile females on his patch that *in spite of* his handicap (his very expensive, long, and cumbersome tail), he has survived, and therefore *because of* his handicap, females should select him as their mate of choice. Zahavi's point is that the size of the handicap will be a true reflection of the total quality of the bird within. In short, *because* of the costs, it can be assumed that the longer the tail, the greater the attraction (the stronger the brand).

It must be said that Zahavi's theory was treated with skepticism by most biologists when first proposed in 1975 to explain why, in societies where males have to compete with each other to be chosen by females, it isn't rare to find the crippling equivalent of a widow bird's tail (e.g., the lion's mane, the Irish elk's antlers). Science accepted that individuals somehow made their hidden qualities known to other individuals and that extreme handicaps could evolve and survive through sexual selection despite being handicaps. To Zahavi's critics, however, it didn't seem to make sense that these expensive advertisements might be favored by selection *because* they were handicaps to the advertisers.

But isn't this what luxury branding is all about? Costly advertising and marketing (including placing the product in quality stores) will add significantly to the final price tag of a product. The producer knows that the higher the end cost of a product, the more exacting will be the end consumer. Therefore, a producer should invest only in top-quality and costly advertising when he is confident in the quality of his own product. If the producer demonstrates that he thinks his product is "worth it," then the consumer can likewise infer that it is "worth it."

Richard Dawkins and John Krebs in "Animal Signals: Information or Manipulation?" (*Behavioural Ecology: An Evolutionary Approach*, Blackwell, 1978, 282–309), argued that it was misleading to try to understand animal signaling by fixating on the idea that animals are trying to convey information.

> If information is shared at all it is likely to be false information, but it is probably better to abandon the concept of information altogether. Natural selection favours individuals who successfully manipulate the behaviour of other individuals, whether or not this is to the advantage of the manipulated individuals.

They suggested that if the word *information* were to be replaced by terms like *manipulation*, *propaganda*, *persuasion*, and *advertising*, one might begin to better understand what is going on when birds sing excessively complicated songs and peacocks display outlandishly exaggerated plumage.

However, and importantly for us business folk who believe in product quality per se, Alan Grafon and others ("Biological Signals as Handicaps," *Journal of Theoretical Biology*, 144 (1990): 517–546) have shown through mathematical modeling that, in evolutionary terms, the best strategy for a courting male to adopt is to honestly signal (display) his true genetic quality by the level of his advertising (by the scale of his handicap), even when this may mean betraying that his true genetic quality is poor. And the best strategy for a female to adopt in this case is to believe what she sees. The point is that there are no long-term benefits for the species in having the male oversell himself to persuade the female that he is more than he is. In due course and further down the line, the truth will come out and his quality will be manifest in his offspring.

In the 1989 edition of his book *The Selfish Gene* (Oxford University Press), Richard Dawkins acknowledges that Grafon's work appears to vindicate Zahavi's theory, which he had dismissed in *The Selfish Gene* when it was first published in 1976. In other words, because the courting male surely must be honest when it comes to selling his story, the female being courted can safely assume that she can judge the contents of his book by its cover.

What about human commerce? I would suggest that the honest signaling strategy adopted by the courting male animal might be usefully applied when branding a product or a company, if we assume that all customers are like the courted female, that is, careful and choosy. Given that a principal aim of branding is to ensure the *longevity* of the brand by establishing a reputation, it makes sense that the quality of advertising (and here I mean packaging, too) should be an honest reflection of the quality of the products for sale under that brand.

Overselling product could well reap rewards in the short term and may be a perfectly sound strategy for a one-season wonder (merchandise produced to coincide with the launch of a film would be an example), but if the product is to endure, if it is to succeed in the long run, it must live up to whatever the consumer has been persuaded to expect of it and it must continue to satisfy a genuine need.

And here's the rub: this concept of *need*. While I am totally convinced that honesty is indeed the best policy when it comes to signaling quality, I am also fully aware that it is perfectly possible for those skilled in the techniques of persuasion to conjure up *need* where none previously existed and then move on to communicate, in all honesty, that they happen to have just the right thing to satisfy that need. In many instances, it's not so much a case of spotting a gap in the market as it is of actively creating one.

The first person ever to make shoes had first to persuade people who had presumably walked happily barefoot for millennia that what they really needed was something to protect their feet, and then to convince them that a shoe would do that job perfectly. Cobblers would then have emerged, dedicated to making different kinds of shoes to suit different kinds of people (men, women, children), who would use them for different purposes—walking, running, and standing around at cocktail parties.

When I devised and launched Jenga, I had neither identified a tower-shaped gap, or niche, in the market that Jenga might fill, nor had I consciously set out to create a *need* that only Jenga might satisfy. However, although Richard Dawkins and his fellow biologists may regard this as a frivolous (mis)appropriation of a profound idea, I would argue now that the very fact that Jenga still survives, that it has so successfully reproduced itself and spawned innumerable similar products, is evidence that the game must satisfy a need, even if neither I nor anyone else can pinpoint precisely what that need might be.

The natural world has plenty more to teach us about creating and fulfilling niches and needs and of employing techniques of persuasion that have been tried and tested over the ages. Turning to botany this time, we find an astonishing variety of methods of signaling (advertising) evolved by plants to attract the specific animals (insects, birds, bats, mice, even monkeys) whose help they now need to transport their pollen grains—the equivalent of sperm—from one of their flowers to another flower of the same species. I say "now need" because, prior to the existence of insects, plants would have pollinated themselves perfectly well, as many still do, relying on the wind or water.

In *The Sex Life of Flowers* (Faber & Faber, 1984), Bastiaan Meeuse and Sean Morris tell us that Christian Konrad Sprengel (1750–1816), "the father of floral biology," was the first to point out that pollinators do not provide their pollen-carrying services free of charge. There must be a quid pro quo; the plant must offer rewards (products) in the form of something the pollinator (the customer, in this case) needs either for its own survival or for that of its offspring. The most common reward, of course, is food, though there are wonderful examples of plants providing shelter. Food can be provided by the pollen itself or, more often, by nectar, which is specifically produced to feed pollinators and thus may be considered a "loss leader" or "marketing expense."

Many flowers advertise themselves and therefore the products they wish to trade by being conspicuous in color, scent, size, and shape, making it possible for their pollinators (their customers) to pick them out from a distance. Then, for close-range interaction with their visitors, the flowers often possess nectar guides in the form of detailed color patterns; Sprengal called them *saftmale*, "juice marks." They are among the most extraordinary examples of just how effectively plants communicate via signage. From the pollinator's viewpoint, many of the patterns displayed within flowers serve as strongly contrasting guidelines (like bright lights on a runway) to direct it to the source of nectar, which may be hidden from view or covered by petals or delicate hairs to shield it from dilution by rainwater. Nectar guides often use colors based on wavelengths that fall outside the range of human vision. The marsh marigold, for example, while appearing a uniform yellow to our eyes, reflects ultraviolet strongly at the tips of its petals but absorbs it totally at the center of the flower, providing a contrast most pollinators would see clearly and recognize as signposting the way to the flower's nectar.

Some plants, such as daisies, are generalists, attracting a wide variety of pollinator customers by means of easily accessible flowers and freely exposed pollen and nectar. Others plants are specialty "shops" focusing on a few customers or even only one.

For example, the flowers of certain evening primroses have such a long, narrow corolla tube that only hawk moths, which have an extremely slender, long, and flexible proboscis, can access the nectar hidden in the tube. Obviously, both partners must benefit from such an arrangement for it to have evolved in the first place. In excluding the majority of other potential pollinators, the evening primrose has greatly increased the chances that the pollen the hawk moth inadvertently collects from its flower will be deposited on a flower of a plant of the same species.

This is because the hawk moth, aware instinctively or from experience that the particularly concentrated high-energy nectar it requires is very likely to be found in the corolla of the evening primrose flower, which it identifies by its color and scent, will visit these flowers in preference to most others. In other words, one might say, the evening primrose commands an enviable level of brand loyalty from its customers, the hawk moths, because it lives up to its brand image, that is, its reputation for supplying the quantity and quality of food that the hawk moths have come to expect. This might be compared to a store loyalty card system by which a customer's loyalty is rewarded and (re)enforced. In this instance, the "store," the plant, cuts down on its costs—the cost of producing too much pollen—because the transfer of its pollen to the right target is assured.

There are even more extreme cases of codependence via coevolution between plants and animals. The more specialized it is, the more rare it is, as this is an increasingly risky strategy. While a high level of interdependence between a plant (product) and its pollinator (customer) may be cost-effective (i.e., energy efficient), if one of the partners were to die out, the other would automatically be doomed. It depends on both always being available for the other. Talk about customer loyalty!

At the extreme end of interdependence, there is an orchid in Madagascar that produces and stores an abundance of a particularly concentrated nectar at the base of an exceedingly long, hollow corolla spur. By examining the flower of this plant (*Angraecum sesquipedale*), Charles Darwin predicted that the plant's pollinator would be a variety of hawk moth, one with a uniquely long proboscis. It took forty years to find this predicted Madagascan orchid's pollinator. When it was finally discovered, it was indeed, as Darwin (and also his contemporary Alfred Russel Wallace) had predicted, a hawk moth—a rare variety of the African hawk moth species—and was duly named *Xanthopan morgani forma praedicta*.

Coevolution of a similar sort exists in the sphere of human commerce. Here, too, extreme interdependency carries with it many of the same rewards, risks, and limitations it does in nature. The toy industry has several examples of this in which major manufacturers and suppliers—for example, Mattel or Hasbro—frequently work in tandem with major retailer chains, in particular Toys "R" Us, on the design of new products. At one time Toys "R" Us represented a whopping 30 percent of the U.S. toy market. Eager to guarantee substantial orders from this giant retail chain, companies such as Mattel would deliberately design product, toys, and games to meet criteria set out by Toys "R" Us. Both sides did this perfectly aware that they risked excluding other retail outlets and limiting the scope of a product. Not surprisingly, given this business model, representatives from Toys "R" Us would often be invited to take part in product-planning sessions. For example, packaging was sized and shaped with a Toys "R" Us shelf in mind to maximize use of display space. The style, layout, colors, and font of the packaging were all designed with a typical Toys "R" Us store and typical Toys "R" Us customer in mind. Even the play element of a game might be jiggled to suit the market, as defined by Toys "R" Us. Games of strategy are impossibly difficult to get into the market in the United States because the major toy buyers believe that Americans prefer games of chance. In summary, one could, from simply looking at the packaging of a toy or game, predict with some certainty when Toys "R" Us shops were its target market—a case of *forma praedicta* perhaps?

Toys "R" Us stores, cavernous warehouses in the main, are audibly as well as visually extremely "noisy" environments. A riot of bold contrasting or clashing colors and emphatic texts crowd the aisles of the stores, deliberately whipping up that fever of excitement we (they) seem to have come to associate with play and childhood. Products that already have to successfully grab the attention of a toy buyer, to get into the store and onto the shelves in the first place, are then required to shout, even scream, to make themselves heard above a general clamor for shoppers' attention.

Yet, despite these deliberate attempts to create a busy, vibrant, hectic atmosphere that is supposed to suggest a huge diversity and choice of product, there is an extraordinary uniformity in the goods available in a Toys "R" Us store. Its shelves are not the place to try to find anything entirely novel. Even in cases where a specific product might be new in itself, it will find its way to a Toys "R" Us shelf only if it is of an already identifiably successful genre. In this environment, niches are filled, not created. For example, once Jenga had become successful, a raft of "stacking games" exploded onto the market: stacking chairs, coins on top of bottles, and many others.

In so many ways Toys "R" Us reminds me of a coral reef and its many brightly colored fishes all jostling for attention, each more vivid than the last in a desperate attempt to stand out from the crowd as well as fit into its chosen milieu.

In summarizing this and the previous chapter on branding, I would say that, despite having "created a game that became a household name," the more I have tried to understand what is involved in building a successful brand, including Jenga, the more I realize that the true mavens of this art might be found way outside the offices of today's business or marketing professional.

If, indeed, as is universally suggested by today's marketing gurus, branding is all about successfully communicating the essence and character of a product or company, then I think we have much to learn from the history of branding (from medieval knights, cattle breeders, tattooists, etc.), as well as from artists (cartoonists, fiction writers, playwrights, etc.) whose livelihoods depend on their skills in succinctly and effectively portraying character. And last but not least, we can learn from animals and plants whose presence and futures depend on communicating the essence of the products they have for sale.

FIFTEEN

Jenga as Metaphor

Metaphorically speaking, metaphors are the building blocks not only of most language but also of most thought. In fact, it has been argued that, quite literally, we humans cannot think abstract thoughts without using metaphor. In other words, the only way we can understand one concept is in terms of another, by applying a word or phrase to an idea that is not meant literally but is used to make a comparison. For example, we like to view life as a journey, and we like to clear and follow pathways to success.

There is a danger of taking this a little too far and believing that nothing exists that cannot be described in relation to some other form of human experience. If this were the case, there would be no such thing as absolute truth or natural law, and science would be just a game, just one narrative among many others. Clearly, this is not so.

There is a whole universe out there that runs according to natural laws totally unaffected by the games we play with words and the metaphors in which we choose to frame our thoughts. Electricity will continue to work the way it works, whether or not we think of it in terms of currents of flowing water (a simile which, by the way, my grandmother took so literally that she would place a bucket under a light socket when she changed a lightbulb to catch and contain any leaks).

Nevertheless, it cannot be denied that because we use language—and here I include art as a kind of language—to communicate with each other, we humans think and live in the metaphors from which language is built. The trick is not to get lost in them, not to allow them to lead us up the garden path, but to make constructive and imaginative use of them in our pursuit of truth in science, literature, and art.

A Constructive Figure of Speech

A well-applied metaphor can help clarify muddled thinking and can even enable an entirely new train of thought, which is why, I believe, artists and scientists are forever hunting down new material for new metaphors.

In this context, Jenga is a gift from the gods! Here is a fresh, concrete, physical, and tangible "concept" that might be applied metaphorically to more abstract concepts without risk of empty platitude. Jenga is well enough known by now for most people to understand the reference to its key feature: instability followed by collapse as a consequence of our activities.

When I put the game Jenga on the market, I had no idea that it would acquire a whole new meaning and become a metaphor, representing a kind of instability that I assume had never before been encapsulated in one word. Of course, I take vicarious pleasure in the game's symbolic role, and I'm perfectly happy as its "author" to bask in reflected glory (metaphorically speaking), but I can't claim that by launching Jenga and picking that word I had any hand in creating the rise of this new metaphor. Be that as it may, the fact is that, today, Jenga metaphors abound.

Jenga in Science

In the article "Food Web Ecology: Playing Jenga and Beyond" (*Science*, July 1, 2005), Peter C. de Ruiter et al. wrote, "Naturalists have long noted that the distribution, abundance, and behaviour of organisms are influenced by interactions with other species" and that an often-used metaphor for the relationship among species was that of the stone arch, with the keystone representing the species that had the dominant role in regulating the structure and stability of the community.

They go on to say that:

> The metaphor of the stone arch might better be replaced with the metaphor of Jenga for although simple rules of balance and energetics govern the stability of both arch and Jenga structures, unlike an arch, a Jenga structure is constantly changing with the additions and deletions of stones and its stability at any moment depends on the importance of a given ingoing or outgoing stone's contribution to the structure.

And several pages later they conclude the article by stating the following:

> The notion of the ecosystem as a static arch has restricted our vision. In contrast, viewing food webs as open and flexible Jenga-like structures that accommodate changes in species composition, attributes and dynamics reveals the features of the ecosystem that are critical to our understanding of community resistance and resilience to environmental change and disturbance.

Note: These excerpts are reprinted with permission from AAAS.

I love the idea that Jenga helped Peter de Ruiter and his colleagues reconsider and perhaps better understand how an ecosystem might work, and I am truly delighted that, in seeing the game from their particular viewpoint, in light of their own expertise and experience, these scientists read considerably more into the game of Jenga than I have, up until now.

Jenga in the Arts

In the online edition of *The Economist*'s quarterly magazine *Intelligent Life*, there was the article, "Jenga and the Art of the Novel," by Emily Bobrow, in which Nathan Englander, author of the novel *The Ministry of Special Cases*, is quoted as saying in a talk that "Fiction writing is kind of a game of Jenga. You sort of have to pull out all the pieces to the point where the story threatens to topple. Just sort of push it to the point where it may collapse. And hope that it doesn't collapse."

Bobrow records that when Englander had finished his talk, she told him that she had found what he had said very interesting. She recalls that he replied, "Really? I was sort of miserable up there," leading Bobrow to conclude her article by observing that "The life of a writer is a game of Jenga, too."

I haven't asked her, but I would guess that Ms. Bobrow, in talking about a "writer," is thinking of a kind of writer rather different from the kind I am, a more artistically tortured soul. But it amuses me to think that my life, now that I'm the writer of the history of the game I devised, *has actually become* that game—metaphorically speaking, of course. It does make me feel rather that I'm trapped in a shaggy-dog story—you know, one of those tales that never end but just keep coming back to their own beginnings.

Artists working in other media have also used Jenga as a metaphor. My mother and I are both Friends of the Royal Academy of Art and always go together to its summer exhibition. For anyone who is not up on the English art or social scene, let me explain that the RA summer exhibition is an annual event dating back to 1769, in which both established and unknown artists exhibit new work throughout the three months of the English summer season. Competition for inclusion is very strong, as there are considerable kudos in having a piece of work selected by the exhibition's curator, a different well-known artist each year.

Five or six summer exhibitions ago, my mother and I came across a large painting entitled "Jenga." It was an impressionistic painting in oils, hazily depicting two women (at least, I think they were women, it was a little hard to tell) in some kind of period Oriental costume seated on cushions playing a game of Jenga, which was positioned on a low table between them. Naturally, I was intrigued by its subject and really wanted to know what had inspired this picture.

Unlike the other exhibitions mounted by the Royal Academy, much of the work in the summer exhibition is for sale, so it wasn't difficult to obtain the name and contact details of the artist who had painted "Jenga." I wrote to him and said that as the inventor of the game, Jenga, I was interested to know the story behind his painting. Why were two women in period Oriental dress playing this modern Western game?

I never heard a squeak in reply. Perhaps I frightened off the artist by expressing proprietorial interest in Jenga. More recently, I came across a website called absolutearts.com, which featured an American artist named Walter King who, inspired by watching a group of friends interacting with each other as they played Jenga in a bar, painted several works based on Jenga, the most interesting of which, I thought, was a Jenga tower constructed of stylized human figures lying on their sides. In the text that accompanied the pictures, he had written, "The game began to suggest all sorts of theatrical and metaphorical relationships about taking risks, survival, economic success and failure, society, politics, friendships and betrayal . . ." and he mentioned that, though not certain, he believed that Jenga might have originated in China, where it was played with pieces of ivory or jade blocks.

Perhaps this misconception was the inspiration behind the painting I saw in England, perhaps it was the other way around, or perhaps

there is just something about the game that had both artists independently looking toward the Orient for clues to its origin. Whatever the
reason in these particular cases, there are countless other examples
of Jenga being used as a springboard for notions whose meanings far
exceed any I might have intended.

Jenga as Inspiration

Moving away from what might be called fine art, there is an increasing number of references to Jenga in the more applied arts, such as in
rhetoric, architecture, and cooking.

In *Art, Argument and Advocacy: Mastering Parliamentary Debate* (International Debate Education Association, 2002), John Meany and Kate
Shuster equate arguing to playing an imaginary game of Jenga using
assumptions rather than wooden blocks.

In *Planning for Disaster* (Kaplan Publishing, 2007) William Ram-
roth states, "There is a marvellous game called Jenga that illustrates
the importance of redundancy in the design of tall buildings." This
concept of redundancy in design may be the inspiration for a building
currently under construction in New York, designed by the architects
Herzog & de Meuron (famous for the Bird's Nest National Stadium in
Beijing), of which it has been said, "It's like a Jenga set come to life"
(designscrapbook.blogspot.com/2008); and ". . . will appear something like a Brobdingnagian stack of glass Jenga pieces" ("First sky-
scraper by Herzog and de Meuron rising in NYC," *Architectual Record*,
September 15, 2008); and "Swiss architects Herzog & de Meuron
revealed their latest design earlier this week: 57 stories of apartments
that emulate a Jenga game . . . in mid-play" ("Beijing's Bird Nest
Architects Reveal Houses Stacked in Manhattan's Sky," *Contractor
Headlines*, September 18, 2008).

Mind you, this is not the first building to have evoked comparison with Jenga. *The Times* online headline said of Frank Gehry's temporary summer pavilion for the Serpentine Gallery in London ("Frank Gehry: the Bilbao Effect is bulls**t" [entertainment.timesonline.co.uk, July 9, 2008]) and that "to the untrained eye it looks like a collapsing tower of Jenga bricks." I'm not sure the unnamed correspondent of *The Times* was being entirely complimentary, but I thought it a fascinating building. I probably would, of course, as I like to think Jenga might have inspired Frank Gehry, a major hero of mine.

Jenga definitely inspired the chef of an Oxford restaurant I went into earlier this year where I discovered "Jenga chips" on the menu. When I asked innocently just what Jenga chips might be, he said, "Oh, they're square-cut potatoes piled like the game," and when I pressed him further by saying, "What game?" he replied, "Jenga, Stupid!" Well, he didn't actually say *stupid*, but he certainly managed to communicate that he thought I was.

There have been some wonderful mixed metaphors using Jenga. In the article by Susan Lang, "Integrating the Web into a Technical Communication Course," the following caught my eye: ". . . an added Web component that might be the piece that brings down the Jenga tower" (Carol Lipson, ed., *Technical Communication and the World Wide Web*, Routledge, 2005, 306). I guess I'm inevitably and uniquely prone to spotting anything that unites the words *Web* and *Jenga* in one sentence, married as I am to a professor of zoology, an arachnologist who spends his life studying spiders and their webs.

Lang continues, "The project is, in itself, an intellectual manifestation of the Jenga game for both instructor and students, challenging them without adding so much in a single turn that one topples the tower" (320). The project referred to here is a class for teaching teachers how to teach techniques of technical writing, for example, when drafting patent applications. I confess, I'm not convinced that the Jenga metaphor in this case helps clarify Lang's message.

Jenga on the Air

There are dozens and dozens of literal and metaphorical references to Jenga in fiction, in novels, on television, and on the big screen. The first time I saw Jenga used in a TV show was some years ago in the British soap opera *Brookside* (no longer extant). In one of the only episodes of the show I ever saw, there was a scene in which the camera was focusing on two people playing a game of Jenga while, out of view and unbeknownst to the players, the boyfriend of one was having his wicked way with the girlfriend of the other. The tower collapsed in a highly symbolic manner at a highly symbolic moment!

A rather less embarrassing and certainly more amusing example of Jenga on screen appeared in the cartoon *Family Guy* with Stewie, the world-weary baby, playing a game with his babysitter. As the game crashes to the ground, Stewie cries "Jengaaaah!" and after a thoughtful pause, adds in his droll upper-class-English voice, "I guess that's why they call it Jenga." This made me laugh out loud. I love the rationale behind this, hinting as it does that Jenga is now a tautology, a word that is, in itself, logically true. The game is called Jenga because it is, by definition, Jenga.

One of my personal favorite sightings of Jenga in fiction is in *Millions*, a wonderful book for children by Frank Cottrell Boyce that was turned into a magical film directed by Danny Boyle in 2005.

Set sometime in the near future, *Millions* is the story of two young brothers who are unwittingly caught up in a train robbery during Britain's countdown to abandoning sterling and adopting the euro as its currency (an as yet wholly fictitious event). Finding themselves suddenly with a vast amount of money in sterling—it literally drops out of the sky when it's flung from a moving train—the boys have the appalling dilemma of how to spend it in the few days left before Britain switches currency and it becomes worthless. While pondering the problem and torn between the vices of buying a million pizzas and the virtues of ending world poverty, the boys play a game with their piles of money that they call "Cash Jenga," which is perhaps as pertinent a metaphor to underscore the themes of the book *Millions* as it would be if used to describe the recent financial crash.

Jenga in Finance

In the article "Financial Jenga: Building up or crashing down?" (*Financial Times Adviser*, October 1, 2008), Emma Hughes writes, "If I am not sorely mistaken I have spotted [that] the polite game of lawn bowls the mortgage industry has been playing for most of this year has swiftly been replaced with what can only be described as financial services Jenga on a global scale."

In case the metaphoric link between Jenga and mortgages is a little too subtle, Hughes adds that, according to Hasbro, the game of Jenga "is a must-have that no fun-loving household would be without."

The article continues to draw parallels between the interdependency of high-street banks and building societies and a game of Jenga and concludes that "soon we will see branches of towering institutions that many thought were unshakeable disappear. Let us hope that does not cause the Jenga tower to come tumbling down on top of us."

Increasingly, Jenga is replacing another game metaphor, that of the game of dominoes, to describe a financial crisis. Perhaps it is because Jenga is a fresher image, but more likely it's because Jenga provides a slightly more useful analogy in those cases in which there is an interdependency of the individual parts of a system.

The domino metaphor better describes a chain reaction, whereby one thing falling knocks over another, which in turn knocks over the next, and so on. I believe first presented as the Domino Theory, this metaphor was coined by President Dwight Eisenhower in 1954 and referred specifically to the effect of communism in Indochina, that is, that if one country in the region were to fall to communism, there would be a follow-on effect in which the next country would fall, and then the next, and so on.

Such a theory is a little ironic, I think, given that dominoes probably originated in China, and more ironic still when you consider that the particular game applied to the situation in metaphor (i.e., lining up a row of tiles and nudging one to cause them all to fall one after the other) is a Western child's toying with a very sophisticated counting game that the Chinese devised several hundred years ago.

Jenga, Games, and the Truth About Business

Aside from Jenga and dominoes, there are almost countless examples of other specific games and sports being used as metaphors, and there is the word *game* itself, of course.

War is a game. Love is a game. Life is a game, and obviously, business is a game. Having been in business for more than twenty-five years and having spent most of that time in the business *of* games, I have to say the business-is-a-game metaphor can be useful provided that it stays just that—a *metaphor*: a point of comparison that should never ever be taken literally or seriously.

There is no satisfactory and universally accepted definitive definition of the word *game*, but I think there is general agreement that a game is a structured activity *separate* from normal life and that the key components of a game, any game, are these:

- It is played within explicit parameters (whether of time or space).
- It involves a challenge and goals.
- It comprises some form of interactivity that is governed by rules unique to that game.

Together, those elements mean that, within the framework of a game, it is totally acceptable to behave in ways that may be seen as truly objectionable in so-called normal life. Tackling and bringing someone crashing to the ground, as you do in rugby, is one such way; bluffing, as you do in many other games, including several I have devised (e.g., Flummoxed, Inspiration, and Ex Libris), is another.

The danger of peddling too hard the idea of seeing business as a game is that it implies that commercial life, like a game, is played out on its own turf, is conducted according to its own set of rules implicitly accepted by all players, and in an arena in which it is perfectly permissible to feign or be economical with the truth.

Groucho Marx might have said in jest that "the secret of success is honesty; once you learn to fake that, you've got it made." Joking apart, faking honesty is often a perfectly legitimate strategy when you're playing to win a game. Dangerously, in thinking of business as a game that you must win, you may deceive yourself that feigning or bluffing is not just acceptable but is actually a positively fair way to play it.

In *Social Evolution* (Benjamin Cummings, 1985), the evolutionary biologist Robert Trivers suggests that various forms of self-deception are common phenomena in humans. He proposes that the evolutionary explanation for this is that an instinct for self-deception can give a person a significant selection advantage. We humans are intuitively very good at detecting when someone is lying to us by "the shifty eyes, sweaty palms and croaky voices" (416). So, if a person genuinely believes his own version of a story, he will be better able to persuade others of its truth because he will not exhibit in his body language any of the usual telltale signs of an attempt to deceive. Trivers turns to psychologists to help explain the mechanisms of self-deception, and he highlights our inclination "to represent ourselves as beneficial and effective at the same time," our propensity "to rewrite past experience so as to make it consistent with present realities" and "a tendency for humans consciously to see what they wish to see." Experiments, he says, have shown that people "literally have difficulty seeing things with negative connotations while seeing with increasing ease items that are positive." We "shunt from consciousness" words and ideas that might otherwise evoke anxiety.

You have only to look at the present economic crisis to witness the effects of self-deception at play. The financial services industry did what one should never do, and it lost its way in a metaphor. It convinced itself and its employees that it was acceptable to think literally of business as a game and therefore entirely legitimate to adopt codes of practice, ethics, appropriate to playing a game. And because most in the industry sincerely believed this themselves, many of their clients and customers were convinced and believed them, too, with the result that in running businesses as though they were playing a game, they ran our economies into the ground.

Another problem with accepting in its entirety the idea that business might be considered a competitive game is the concept of equality. Almost without exception, games are by their very nature competitive. However, built into the idea of competition in most games is the concept of a level playing field. The paraphernalia of a game is designed to afford each player an equal chance. Only through superior skill or blind luck can you win, not because you play by biased rules or because you start out with more playing pieces than your opponent, or because the dice are loaded in your favor. Inequality renders a game dull. For this reason, games such as geese and fox are no longer played, except by young children or as historic curiosities, for in this example the fox has the much greater chance and invariably wins. Most classic games that are still played today have evolved by ironing out these issues. Thus, a game of chess starts with balanced armies of pieces, and each player starts with the same sum of money in Monopoly and with the same quantity of letter tiles, selected at random, in Scrabble.

Not so in business. Yes, there is a concept of "unfair competition" within the world of trade and commerce, and there are some rules of engagement, with referees (government agencies) to pull us up when we cross the line—but the rules governing a free market economy are not equivalent to the rules of a game. One of the primary purposes of the rules of a game is to define when that game ends and hence when there is a return to reality. But business *is* always reality, and there are no rules that call a stop to the action and release all players from the game and their losses.

In my introduction, I equate starting and running a business with taking a journey or playing a game. In doing this, I liberally and unashamedly mix those two metaphors as a way of trying to order and to express my thoughts. I don't intend for either metaphor to be taken literally. I don't think I have ever entirely confused playing a game, or taking a journey, with real life. However, because I have always liked playing games and have always liked traveling (a form of play in its own way), I think through travel and through playing games I have learned much about myself (certainly my limitations), about other people, and about the world around me, which I probably apply to many aspects of real-life challenges, if albeit unconsciously.

Johan Huizinga (the cultural historian I introduced in chapter 6) considered our instinct for play so fundamental an element of human culture as to suggest we should be called *Homo Ludens*—Man the Player—and he adds that what characterizes the very essence of play is *fun*. But there he leaves us dangling, claiming that the *fun* of play resists all analysis, all logical interpretation.

Well, I would like to offer at least one interpretation of what is meant by the *fun* of play, in suggesting that this fun derives from the exciting *freedom* play grants us to temporarily step outside real life and to take risks. Only with such freedom can we play with ideas, play with words, or put thought experiments to the test, all safe in the knowledge that regardless of the outcome, no real-life harm will be done.

Although it may be the fun that games offer that appeals to us, serious lessons can be learned from the experience of playing games.

Challenging games that mimic facets of real life can hone certain skills, sharpen strategic thinking, encourage innovation and creativity, engender team spirit, and, above all, help us recognize and appreciate a certain kind of fun, the genuine, liberating *fun of play*—playful fun that isn't bought at anyone else's expense.

If, as Huizinger says in *Homo Ludens*, our instinct for play drives and nourishes all human endeavor, it is entirely natural that we might wish to see business as a journey or a game and to consider taking risks and meeting challenges as exciting and fun. Well, maybe we can and maybe we should equate business with a game. But if we do so, then we must, all along the way and however rough the ride, keep a firm grasp on reality and never ever forget that in real life, unlike a game, the consequences of our actions will be real, and more especially, will continue to affect real people long after the end of play.